1,001 Boredom Busting Play Ideas

Free and Low Cost Crafts, Activities, Games, and Family Fun that Will Help You Raise Happy, Healthy Children

Jean Oram

WARNING! Author and/or publisher do not take responsibility for any loss, damage, and/or injury as a result of following or trying activities in this book. Please play safe. Follow your gut. Always talk to an adult before engaging in new play activities. Don't play with fire. Don't run with scissors. And always follow your family's rules about safety.

Interior photo credits and copyright: Jean Oram
Cover and interior design Jean Oram

1,001 Boredom Busting Play Ideas:
Free and Low Cost Crafts, Activities, Games, and Family Fun that Will Help You Raise Happy, Healthy Children

For more information contact Jean Oram at JeanOramBooks@gmail.com. www.JeanOram.com www.itsallkidsplay.ca
Printed in the United States of America unless otherwise stated on the last page of this book. Published by Oram Productions Alberta, Canada.

LIBRARY OF CONGRESS CATALOGING-IN-PUBLICATION DATA
Oram, Jean.
1,001 Boredom Busting Play Ideas: Free and Low Cost Crafts, Activities, Games, and Family Fun that Will Help You Raise Happy, Healthy Children / Jean Oram.—1st. ed.
    p. cm.
  ISBN: 978-1-928198-22-2 (paperback)
  Ebook ISBN: 978-1-928198-05-5
1. Play. 2. Parenting. 3. Early Child Education - - Activity programs. 4. Crafts and Hobbies / Crafts for Children. 5. Games - - Travel Games. 6. Games - - Reference. 7. Child Development. 8. Child Rearing. 9. Parent and Child. 10. Handicraft. 11. Crafts for Children. I. Title.

Summary: Over 1,000 play ideas including travel games, classic group games, outdoor games, family playdate ideas, birthday party games, sleepover ideas, crafts for children, math games, reading fun, tricky challenges, and sensory play ideas. (And much more free play fun touted by child development experts.) Let's have fun! Let's play!

First Oram Productions Edition: December 2015

DEDICATION

For my kids, of course. Thanks for playtime—this book wouldn't have happened without you both.

But also to my first playmate, my brother, Jonathan. You taught me a lot about life, the universe, and everything.

Also, to my parents and the village of Swalwell. It took a village to raise me and the other 'ragamuffins,' and I wouldn't have it any other way.

And finally, to Neil Salkind for leading me to the science.

For those about to laugh and play, I salute you.

CONTENTS

CONTENTS CONTINUED

Play has been recognized by the United Nations High Commission for Human Rights as the right of every child.

THE ESSENCE OF LIFE: PLAY

Life without play is a grinding, mechanical existence organized around doing the things necessary for survival. Play is a stick that stirs the drink. It is the basis of all art, games, books, sports, movies, fashion, fun and wonder—in short, the basis of what we think of as civilization. Play is a vital essence of life. It is what makes life lively.

Stuart Brown, Play

WHY YOU MIGHT NEED THIS BOOK

Kids:

Are you so bored…

1) Your legs and arms feel sooo heavy you have to drag them?

2) Nothing in the world could ever be exciting again—maybe even ice-cream? <Gasp>

3) When you talk, your words come out like this: "I'm sooooo booooorrrrreeeedddd."

If you nodded weakly to any of the above questions, you need this book. Take it to the nearest checkout along with your allowance or an adult with money. Now. Run. Go! Go! As long as this book is in your possession you will never be bored again! I guarantee it.

Adults:

You need this book if:

1) You have come to believe having a string of green lights on the way to your son's/daughter's soccer/dance/hockey/karate/boy scout/other activity is "fun" for the whole family.

2) It has been more than 10 years since you rolled in the grass rendered useless by an attack of the giggles.

Okay, okay. I'm being a bit silly. (Not really.) Here are some *real* reasons an adult needs this book:

1) *1,001 Boredom Busting Play Ideas* will make you a better parent. Seriously. You can hand your kids this book of activities instead of gritting your teeth and tuning out their "I'm so bored" pleas. Or worse—paying huge amounts of money for a barely tolerated afterschool activity that makes you a taxi driver every night of the work week.

If you're a caregiver or babysitter, this book will save you during those moments when your charges are looking at you for entertainment and your mind blanks out or they begin to rebel against your usual arsenal of activities. <Shudder>

2) *1,001 Boredom Busting Play Ideas* is cheaper than an afterschool activity. Plus, you don't have to drive. Well, no promises on that, actually. But you can always say "no" if they ask you to drive them to the beach. With over 1,000 activities, you can find something entertaining that doesn't involve driving or you getting off the couch.

3) Free, unstructured play (where kids make the rules and use their imagination) is an integral part of the emotional, physical, and cognitive development in children. It also promotes problem-solving skills as well as creativity. (Sounds pretty good doesn't it? Well, that's the stuff this book is jam-packed with.)

4) *1,001 Boredom Busting Play Ideas* is FUN.

5) No more, "I'm bored."

6) Adults enjoy *1,001 Boredom Busting Play Ideas,* too.

7) Kids learn by doing (playing) and *1,001 Boredom Busting Play Ideas* has a ridiculous amount (actually 1,028! I added some bonus activities) ways to get your kids up and active, no matter what their interests happen to be.

8) *1,001 Boredom Busting Play Ideas* will bring you and your family closer when you do these activities together. Families that spend quality time together playing and communicating have a lowered risk of breaking up. As well, children of families that spend quality time together have better social skills, get better grades, and are more resistant to alcohol and drug-related pressures.

9) The activities in *1,001 Boredom Busting Play Ideas* will create a lifetime of family memories when done together as a family.

So, pick up this book and go have some fun!

WHAT IS PLAY?

Play: A naturally occurring activity among children, often used as a way to entertain and amuse themselves. Play is used by children to learn about themselves and their world. By pretending and practicing life (playing), children learn about their personal environment, relationships, and culture, as well as their society's norms, values, and much more. Play is essential for proper child development (psychological, physical, and cognitive). *Free Play:* An unstructured, spontaneous way of discovering one's world and one's self. Free play is key to child development and is commonly responsible for developing problem-solving skills and creativity in children. And while it may appear as though a child is doing "nothing productive," they are actually learning while experimenting with their world, society, and culture—all in ways that other types of play do not.

Structured Play: Activities for children organized by adults with the distinct goal of being educational and thought-provoking. Rules and structure are in place. There is often little room for self-expression, creativity or the development of imagination.

Scripted Toys and Play: Some toys (often licensed—tied-in with movies, TV shows, etc.) come with a predetermined script and work in certain ways. Scripted toys leave little opportunity for children to determine how the toys are played with, or allow them to apply their own personal expression to the play script.

An example: Give a stick to ten different children and chances are they will use it in ten different ways. That stick could be a gun, walking stick, shovel, something for jumping over, magic wand, etc. Give them a magic wand that lights up and chances are that it will not be used as a gun, walking stick, shovel, or something for jumping over. It is a magic wand. All forms of play are important for healthy child development, however in recent North American society, free play has become severely undervalued while scripted and structured play have become overvalued. This book is full of ideas on how to ditch the structure, schedule, and script, and integrate free play in your child's life once again—whether you have five minutes or five days.

Let's play!

FOREWORD

There are psychological consequences to not engaging in spontaneous
self-initiated play.

David Elkind
The Power of Play

The activities in this book focus on unstructured, unscripted, and unscheduled, child-directed "free play"—play that is necessary for healthy child development. (Free play is essentially the form of play we engaged in when we were kids and is becoming increasingly rare in today's plugged in, busy world.) Yet, research has found that free play not only lays the foundation for real life and real life learning (it is how the human brain evolved to learn), but it is also a way for children to develop at their own pace and without pressure. By playing freely (without adult organization and adult structuring, in other words, child directed), healthy brain development is promoted in children of all ages.

Free play has been linked to the development of the following skills and abilities: problem solving, creativity, communication, conflict resolution, self-confidence, critical thinking, personal resiliency, intellectual curiosity, social competency, emotional control, decision making, empathy, self-advocacy, leadership, a sense of fairness and justice, freedom of expression, and the discovery and development of personal interests and passions. According to the current science in the areas of parenting and brain development, children who engage in free play have a greater understanding of the world around them, higher grades, better classroom behavior, as well as lowered incidences of ADHD, childhood depression, anxiety, and childhood obesity; all things children need in order to be active, healthy, productive, and thriving citizens of today's world.

As children in developed countries continue to see a reduction in time permitted to engage in free play, we see its negative impact on their social, psychological, cognitive, emotional, and physical development. Increased over-scheduling and screen time (TV, video games, computers, and smart phones), reduced recess time, and the pressure to enroll our children in numerous extracurricular activities, as well as a generalized fear of letting our children roam outside to play are all contributing to rising rates of childhood obesity, depression, anxiety, ADHD, as well as children lacking independence skills (you could read that as bubble-wrapped kids). We mean well. We want our children to be as safe as possible and we try to curb risk-taking behavior. We keep them inside, believing our neighborhoods aren't safe and that putting them in organized sports is a viable solution. But often these sports are very prescribed (they play at a certain time, at a certain place, with certain other children). The sport becomes an obligation rather than true play. We no longer allow children to decide when they want to participate and when they want to stop—in effect, teaching them that we know their needs and wants best so they need not bother to listen to them as they surely won't be correct in their assessment. According to the science, the simplest and healthiest thing we can do to combat and prevent these alarming health issues in our children is to foster opportunities for them to engage in child-directed free play as well as encourage more outdoor play time. It's that simple.

Lately, an increasing number of organizations are being created to promote and preserve free play. As well, more documentaries are being aired that argue for longer recesses (recesses have been removed in up to 40% of American schools despite studies demonstrating that adequate recess time leads to higher test scores—not increasing the time spent in front of teachers). Documentaries also show how free play is being incorporated in childhood programs with beneficial results, and that playgrounds are being redesigned to encourage free play and mild risk-taking. In general, we have been overprotecting our children, which is, in turn, limiting the development of skills they need in order to be successful in our ever-changing and challenging world.

The amazing thing about this problem is that the solution is so simple. How can something so basic as unstructured play work? That's the beauty and complexity of the evolved human brain. We take it for granted and yet every second it is doing amazing, complex things—and especially when engaging in free play. The best part about free play is that children can participate anywhere, anytime, and for free. Free play activities are smart by nature and promote and foster healthy brain development every single time. What could be smarter than that?

And yet, many parents are feeling uncertain about where and how to start making changes in their children's lives—what if they mess it up? Shouldn't there be a guidebook? Shouldn't they be assigned a wingman when they're handed their newborn?

Parents, meet your wingman. *1,001 Boredom Busting Play Ideas* will be the encouraging partner telling you it's possible and to trust yourself. Just open a page and go for it. It's that easy. I'm right there with you. Follow your heart. It won't steer you wrong.

You got this.

Jean Oram
Alberta, Canada

2015

WHO GOES FIRST GAMES

Sometimes the hardest part about playing with others is deciding who's going to be "it" first. Fear not! If your kids are still working on their compromising skills then this section will help them out.

Flip a Coin

Flip a coin (quarters are a good size) in the air and catch it with one hand. Without opening that hand, lay it flat on top of the other hand for the coin's "reveal." Is it heads or tails? Heads is the side with the person's head, tails is the side with the animal (or other object).

Keep track of how often it lands heads and how often it lands tails. Is it the same number?

This is a great way to decide which team goes first in a team game. You can also play the coin flipping game with a friend (or alone) where they have to "call it" while the coin is still in the air. Were they right? How often do they guess right?

Eeny Meeny, Miney Moe

While picking a person to be "it" or to make a choice when you can't decide, sing this song:

Eeny, meeny, miny, moe,
Catch a tiger by the toe.
If he hollers let him go,
Eeny, meeny, miny, moe.
*You are not it. (Variation: You **are** it.)*

As you say each word, point to one of the choices (people). If you are singing the "not it" version, the one pointed to when you say "it" is out. Keep going until you have one person left.

Who is the Youngest/Oldest

Youngest/oldest person goes first, depending on which one the group has chosen.

Tallest/Shortest

Tallest or shortest person goes first.

Who Won/Lost

The person who won/lost last time gets to go first or be it.

Next Birthday

Who's birthday is next? They get to go first. If it is their birthday—they go first.

Call It
Starting a game of tag? Everyone immediately yells "not it!" The last person to say "not it" is it.

Pick a Number
One person agrees to think of a number between 1 and 10 and keeps it to themselves—they don't tell anyone. Everyone else guesses a number between 1 and 10. The person who guesses the right number or guesses closest to the right number gets to go first. If there is a tie, then those who tied guess again.

The person choosing the number can also write it down in case you think they might change their mind!

Pick a Name Out of a Hat
Write everyone's name down on scraps of paper—one name per piece of paper. Put all the names in a hat (or whatever you've got handy). Shake them around to mix them up, then draw one name out. The person who's name is pulled out is "it" or goes first.

Variation: Don't have paper and a pencil? How about rocks? Put rocks that are almost the same in a hat and make one of the rocks different somehow—like its color—and the person who draws that rock gets to be "it."

Draw Straws
You will need one straw for each person. Make one of the straws shorter than the others. One person holds the straws in a clump so nobody can tell which is the shorter one. Everyone pulls one straw—the person with the shortest straw is "it" or goes first.

Variation: If you don't have straws, how about twigs, or dandelion stems?

Rock, Paper, Scissors
Two players make a fist. On the count of three everyone reveals rock, paper or scissors. Rock beats scissors (smashes it). Scissors beats paper (cuts it). Paper beats rock (covers it).

To make a rock, make a fist. To make paper, lay your hand flat. To make scissors do the peace sign but with your hand pointing sideways (pointer finger and middle finger pointing straight out of a fist).

This is a fun way to decide who goes first when playing a new game.

Flip a Coin

Toss a coin in the air. While it is in the air, one of two players/teams calls the coin. (They choose heads or tails.) If it lands with the animal/building/landmark side up, it is tails. Heads is the side with the human on it. If they are correct, they get to choose whether to go first or not.

Bubble Gum, Bubble Gum

Bubble gum, bubble gum in a dish, how many bubble gums do you wish?

On each word of the chant above, the person singing the song taps one person's fist with theirs, going around the circle of players as they go. (The person tapping also taps their own fist.) The person who is tapped when they say "wish," then chooses a number between 1 and 5. The person leading counts it out, tapping fists as they go. The person who they land on for chosen number is now out. Keep going until there is one person left. The last person left (not out) goes first.

Closest Number Wins

Number of players: 3 or more.

One player chooses a number in their head, but doesn't tell the others—only what number range it is in. For example: I'm thinking of a number between 1 and 100.

The other players try to guess closest to the number, but only have one guess. Whoever guessed closest to the number wins/goes first/isn't "it"/is "it."

TRICKY BODY CHALLENGES

> Children need to actively explore the world with his body and through his senses.
>
> David Elkind
> The Power of Play

By challenging ourselves to attempt the undoable (try touching your elbows together behind your back) we develop self-awareness while creating intellectual curiosity. Why *can't* we touch our elbows behind our backs?

As well, challenging ourselves in a play environment creates an impact-free setting where we can experience failures (and successes) while learning about ourselves, our limitations, and our world. Children who learn to deal with failure tend to more resilient. So, let's test ourselves in a healthy, fun, and goofy way!

You: Without Thumbs
What can you do without thumbs? What do you think would be easy? Difficult?

Have someone gently tape your thumbs to the side of your hand. Try different things like tying your shoes, writing your name, and picking up a teddy bear with no thumbs to help you out. Can you get the tape off again without help? It's tricky!

Toes as Fingers
Place a pencil or paint brush between your toes and draw or paint a picture. Can you do it? What do your drawings and paintings look like? Can you write your name?

Mouth as Fingers
Similar to the activity above, instead of using fingers to hold your pencil or paintbrush, try holding it in your mouth. Is that easier or harder than using your toes?

Who Smelt It Dealt It
Armpit farts—scentless flatulence. To make a good armpit fart that sounds real, place your right hand in your bare left armpit. (Or your left hand in your right armpit if that's more comfortable.) Hook your thumb outside your armpit so it is pointing up towards your shoulder. Then quickly move your left arm up and down to make a farting noise in your armpit. It might take a bit of practice, but it will be well worth it when you impress your friends.

Note to boys: Boys are generally more impressed with this trick than girls—girls just don't seem to understand the pure joy of making a fart sound, so don't be discouraged if girls give you an eye roll.

Note to girls: Boys LOVE a girl who can make a good armpit fart and they'll be a great audience for your new trick.

Lick Your Nose Some people can, some people can't. Can you?

Well, don't give up! Keep trying! And if you can… how high can you get with your tongue? (Just, um, not up your nose, okay? Nobody wants to see that. Well, maybe. Just once though so we can be disgusted while being suitably impressed.)

Wiggle Your Eyebrows
Wiggle your eyebrows—both of them, now try just one. Can you do it?

Wiggled Your Ears
Can you do it?

Wiggle Your Nose
I can do this one! Like a rabbit smelling a yummy carrot. Can you do it?

Wink
Can you wink with just one eye? How fast can you switch between winking one eye, then the other?

Ha Ha! That's a Funny Laugh How many different laughs can you make up? How about a snorting laugh? A high giggle? A low guffaw? Are there some laughs that make you laugh for real?

Did you know: Laughter is called the best medicine because it makes us feel better (want to change your mood—laugh! Even fake laughs can turn your mood right around). Plus, laughter can help ward off a cold! Is that cool, or what?

Burp The Alphabet Try to make your burps sound like letters of the alphabet. Fake burps can count, because, hey, the alphabet is 26 burps long! By the way, stop if you feel like you're going to hurl. It would just be yucky if you did that.

Curl Your Tongue Can you curl up the side edges of your tongue so they almost touch each other?

Some people can do this one and some people can't. Can you? I've heard that if your parents can do it, you should be able to, too, as it's hereditary. Can they curl their tongue?

Talk With Your Mouth Closed My parents used to say this by accident all the time while trying to get my brother and I to not talk with our mouth full of food during meal time.

To do this… uh… well, keep your lips together and talk! See if people can understand you. Are some words or sounds harder to say than others?

Balance a Book on Your Head
Can you walk with a book on your head? Sit? Walk up and down stairs? (Without holding the book and without it falling off, of course.) Some people will say you have amazing posture if you can do this without the book falling off.

Cross Your Eyes—They Won't Freeze That Way (I Hope) If you can't cross your eyes, try this: Take a finger and hold it way out in front of your nose. Focus both eyes on your finger, then slowly bring the finger in until it touches your nose. If you've kept both eyes focused on that finger, guess what? You've gone cross-eyed! Congratulations. Let's hope they don't freeze like that.

Tongue Twisters
Can you say these tricky phrases 10 times each, really fast, without messing up?

Mass at the Mosque
Toy Boat
The skunk said the stump stunk.
She sells seashells at the seashore.

Can you make up your own tongue twisters? What do you think makes a good tongue twister? (What is it that makes tongue twisters so difficult to say?)

Coin Catching à la Elbow!
Put your right hand on your right shoulder. Point your elbow out in front of you. Lay a penny on the flat part of your arm just above your elbow. Without moving your arm, turn your hand so the palm of your hand is facing up. Very quickly move your elbow down and try to catch the falling penny with your right hand.

The record for caught pennies when I was a kid was a stack of 14. How many can you catch?

Note: Do you live in Canada where they did away with pennies a few years ago? Try this trick with dimes instead!

Light as a Feather, Stiff as a Board
One player lays stiffly (not relaxed) on the ground with 4-6 other players around them. The other players place their index (pointer) fingers under him or her. The players all say together, "Light as a feather, stiff as a board," twenty times. Then they start pushing up with their fingers and for the player on the floor it should feel as though they are being lifted (even though they are still on the ground).

Spoonerific Want to know the secret trick to hanging a spoon off your nose? Rub the scoop part of the spoon until it has some oil from your fingers on it. It might also help to breathe on the scoop and then rub. This will help create friction on the spoon's smooth surface. (Friction makes it stick and not slide off much.) Then take the spoon and place the scoop part on the end of your nose.

Did it work? If not, also try rubbing the spoon gently over the end of your nose. Sometimes the natural oils from your nose helps make it stick.

Can you stick it to other parts of your face? Your ears? Cheeks? Chin? Upper lip?

Fun facts: Guess who holds the world record for the most spoons on their face at a time? It's a kid! (17 spoons!) And the record for the longest amount of time for having one spoon hanging off a nose was two hours! How about you? Can you break any records?

Pencil Tricks
Can you hold a pencil between your upper lip and your nose? How about between your lower lip and your chin? Can you balance it on your ear? Nose? How about on your eyebrows? Where else?

Pat Your Head & Rub Your Tummy The trick to this one is to start doing one—like patting your head—and once that is going smoothly, add in rubbing your stomach. Good luck! It's trickier than it sounds. I can do it if I pat with my left, but if I pat with my right… it just doesn't work at all.

Lick Your Elbow
Can you reach the end of your elbow with your tongue? I can't, but I once met a kid who can.

Touch Elbows—Together Behind Your Back
I can't do this one either! How about you? Have you met anyone who can? I haven't yet, but I'm still looking. I wonder why people can't seem to do this one… do you know why?

Finger Toes Can you pick things up with your toes? Start with something easy and smooshy like socks, then move on to harder objects like a pencil.

Tip: Use bare feet! Although bonus points if you can pick things up with your toes while wearing socks.

Monoped

A monoped is a person with one leg.

No, no, don't take off a leg, silly—you are going to need two for the next activity! Balance on one leg—pretend the other leg isn't there. (Or tie your legs together or simply keep them tight together like they are one leg.) Can you hop and bounce around without falling over or using both legs to save you? It's tricky—be careful. It is easy to fall over in a nasty and not so graceful way.

What can you do? Can you make it all the way around the living room? Can you still play hopscotch? Which leg is easier to hop around on?

Jumping Jacks

How many jumping jacks can you do in a row before your legs feel as though they're going to fall off? Can you do as many as your parents or sibling?

Walk Backwards

How fast can you go? Is it easy or hard to turn corners into other rooms? Can you jump over things? Can you walk up stairs? (You might want to hold on to the railing while testing that one for the first time.)

Click Your Heels

Jump in the air and click your heels together off to your left or right side. Can you do it? Just on one side or can you do both sides?

Crazy Arms

Stand in a doorjamb with your arms down at your sides. Push the tops of your hands against the doorjamb. Push as hard as you can for one minute. Step out of the doorjamb and slowly relax your arms. They should feel like they're going to lift themselves all by themselves.

Crazy Legs

On the floor, lie on your back. Have someone hold your legs about 2 feet (60 cm) off the floor. Relax your legs completely so the other person is holding up your legs and you are just chilling out, not using a muscle. Wait one minute. Then, have your partner slowly, slowly, slowly let your legs down to the floor. It should feel like your legs are going right through the floor! How crazy is that?

Move Objects With Your Mind
Can you move that pencil on the desk just by thinking about it? How about a feather? Does it help if you concentrate really hard? Make a funny face? (Don't worry, I can't move things either. What? You can!? Whoa! That's amazing!)

Moonwalk
Moonwalking is cool because it looks like you're walking forward, but you're actually sliding backwards!

The trick to moonwalking is to never let your toes or the balls of your feet (the cushy part of your foot between your toes and the arch) ever leave the ground. To move, bend your right knee and come up onto the ball of your right foot. Slide your flat left foot back without letting any part of it come off the ground. This is important: Make sure you keep your whole left foot on the ground as you slide it back—no lifting your heel. Now, switch feet and do it all again. You're moonwalking!

Tip: Wear socks so you slide better. It's all about the slide…

Handy Nose
Can you move cotton balls with your nose just by breathing?

Inhale (breathe in) through your nose above a cotton ball to pick it up. Keep inhaling in until you want to drop it. Be careful—it tickles! See how many you can move from one pile to another in 30 seconds. (Got the skill mastered? Challenge a friend or sibling to a race!)

Want to mix it up? How about an exhaling race? Breathe out through your nose on the cotton ball (mouth closed!) and see how far and fast you can move it.

Nose Races
Using only your nose, nudge a tennis ball along the floor and try to beat the other racers across the finish line.

Snap Your Fingers
Use your middle finger and your thumb for this one. You sort of push them together fairly hard, then let them slip off each other sideways—making a snapping sound.

Mouth Sounds

How many different sounds can you make with your mouth? Click your tongue? Make cork popping sounds? Clicks? Knocking sounds?

Spit Bubbles

Okay, I'll warn you. This one can be kind of disgusting—I'm almost embarrassed to put this one in here—but they're kind of fun, and what's childhood without making a spit bubble or two… or fifty.

Careful not to drool on yourself… Here's what you do. Gather a bunch of saliva (spit) in your mouth—don't swallow it. Then scoot that saliva to the front of your mouth so you can play with it using the tip of your tongue. Play around with your breath and your tongue to see if you can make bubbles.

Climb a Doorjamb

"Walk" up a doorjamb by using the sides of the doorjamb. Place one hand on the hinge side of the doorframe and the other hand on the latch side. Put a foot on each side as well. Push out really hard with your arms and legs so you don't slip down (bare feet will give you extra grip), and slowly move your hands and feet up, one at a time until you have climbed to the top. My poor mom was always having to wipe our hand and footprints off the doorjambs when we were kids. Sorry Mom!

Bonus: When you reach the top of the doorjamb, try doing a chin-up by holding onto the top of the doorjamb and pulling yourself all the way up until your shoulder touches the top of the doorjamb. Where do you go now? Gotta go down and try it again!

TRICKY BUSINESS

Play is a central component in children's mental growth. Play helps children make meaning in their world, it helps them learn about themselves, and equally crucially, it helps them learn how to get along with others.

Kathy Hirsh-Pasek, Roberta Michnick Golinkoff, & Diane Eyer
Einstein Never Used Flashcards

Biggest Gum Bubble in the World Can you blow a gum bubble big enough that it covers your nose when it pops? Try it. Maybe you can break a world record and make the biggest gum bubble EVER!

Tip: You need lots of gum to blow a good bubble. Soft cubes of gum like Bubbalicious, Hubba Bubba, and Bubble Yum work well. Question is: Is your mouth big enough?

Hula Hoop Count how many times (or for how long) you can keep the hoop spinning around your waist. What about around one leg? An arm? How many times? Can you beat your own records? What about more than one hoop at a time? How about you and your friends? Who rocks the hula hoop? (Maybe it's Dad!)
Tip: You need a good hula hoop that has a bit of weight to it to do this one well. (A lot of the pretty ones they sell for kids aren't very good for hula hooping—what on earth were they thinking? It's called a hula hoop, people!)

Change The Rules
If you could change the rules to your favorite (or least favorite game—it can be a board game or an active game), what rules would you change? Try it! Maybe you just made the game even better!

Baby Giggles
There is nothing like making someone else giggle, and babies are great for this. They love to laugh at the craziest things! What does it take to make the baby in your life giggle? Peek-a-boo? Soft touches on the nose with a favorite teddy bear? Pretending to fall down? Tickles? (Okay, even I laugh at those last two!)

It's Shocking!
Give someone a shock. ZAP!

This works best when it's winter and the air is dry. While wearing socks, drag your feet across the carpet, then touch someone. Zap! Did you get a shock too? Try it again, does it work every time? (And as tempting as it is, don't touch poor kitty on the end of the nose. Ouch!)

Learn...
- • To Tie a New Knot (and untie it—Oops!)
- • A Card Trick
- • A Magic Trick

Pet Talk
What would your pet say if he or she could talk? Wait… maybe your pet *can* talk….

Have a conversation with your pet! Listen to the sounds your pet makes while watching their body language (what they do with their body—it's a way of speaking). Ears up means they're curious and listening. Ears down flat—uh, oh! They are either getting ready to pounce or they are angry or scared. What else does your pet say?

Furry animals are great when it comes to body language. But lizards, snakes, and fish? Well, they are a little trickier to figure out. Can you guess what they're thinking, feeling, or saying?

Teach Your Pet Tricks
Even cats can learn tricks. I taught my cat to jump through a hoop, sit on a chair, roll over, shake a paw, sit up, and lie down. No, really. I did! And no, he wasn't a dog dressed up like a cat.

Be gentle, patient, and reward your pet with their favorite treat while you are training them—even if they don't get the trick all the way right. It may take a few weeks of training for your pet to learn one trick. Work on the trick a few times every day for a few weeks. Once they have one trick figured out, begin teaching them another one. Before long, your pet will be able to put on a whole show!

Lava!
There are different variations for this game, but the main idea is that the ground is covered in hot lava so you'd better not touch it. Ah! Watch out!

Feet can't touch the floor: You can touch the floor, but not with your feet. Walk on your hands, roll, or slither on your stomach.

None of your body can touch the floor: Use cushions, blankets, furniture, or paper as safe stepping stones so your feet don't touch the lava. If you're outside you can use leaves— don't let your feet touch the grass. You can make paths to walk on, long jumps to take, as well as add other obstacles to make it more challenging.

What other versions of this game can you create?

Note: You can play this one alone or with a group of people!

Scary Flashlight Faces

A good place to do this is in front of a mirror in a dark place like a bathroom. Place the flashlight under your chin and shine it up to make shadows on your face. Make scary and weird faces. Does the flashlight make you look stranger?

Give it a try...
- • Make Funny Faces in the Mirror (no flashlight required for this one)
- • Make a Crazy Hairdo
- • Sticker Yourself with Stickers
- • Rub on Fake Tattoos (or draw some with washable markers)
- • Make Up Jokes

Chin Puppet

You will need: face paint, a tea towel or bandana, and probably someone to help unless you have some pretty amazing upside-down-drawing-on-your-face skills, an audience, and a couch, stage or bed.

A chin puppet is an upside down face puppet. Your mouth will be your chin puppet's mouth, but your chin will be the puppet's forehead and face. (When your head is upside down, the puppet will be right side up.)

After you or someone else has painted a face on your chin (eyes, eyebrows, nose, and maybe a mustache), place a tea towel (or bandana) over your real eyes and nose so your mouth and chin are showing. Lie on something like a bed or a couch where you can hang your head over the edge. You will be looking at everything upside down and your puppet will be right side up. Now sing a song or tell a joke for your audience. If they don't laugh there is seriously something wrong with them.

52 Card Pick-Up

Take a full deck of playing cards and throw them in the air. Then pick them up. That's 52 Card Pick-Up. (Ask a friend if they want to play. Tell them you'll deal.)

Paper Bag Bang!

Bunch the opening of a paper bag so you can blow into it, filling it with air. Hold the bag tightly closed with one hand, then bang hard on the bottom to make it burst. When it breaks, it will make a loud bang.

Yowzers! That's loud. I bet you scared someone!

Take Something Apart
Make sure you ask your parents if it is okay before you start. And if it is an electronic use your noggin and unplug it first. What's inside? What parts are there? Can you figure out what they do?

Fix Something
Can you solve why this broken thing doesn't work any longer? Maybe it needs batteries, cleaning, or a new part. (Be sure to ask your parents first before taking something apart even if it's broken.)

As a kid I took a broken iron apart, certain I could fix it. I couldn't, but it was an interesting project. There were so many mysterious pieces in there! Since then I've taken other things apart… and wait for it… fixed them! We all have to start somewhere.

House of Cards
Build a house out of playing cards by stacking them on their edges. See if you can use the whole deck. Or… try making a house that is bigger than four cards before it falls down. Don't laugh. It's trickier than it sounds!

Indoor Fort
Big cushions (like off the couch—excuse me Mom, but I'm making a fort), large cardboard boxes, chairs, and bed sheets are great for making an indoor fort.

Now that you have a fort, what are you going to do inside it? Have a tea party? Hold special club meetings? Tell jokes? Sleep? Read?

Upside Down World
Lie on your back on the couch or on your bed. Hang your head over the edge and ta-da! The world is upside down. Don't doorways look really strange? What if your house was upside down all the time?

Obstacle Course
Make an obstacle course out of pillows, blankets, laundry baskets, cardboard, string, or whatever you have handy. In an obstacle course, you need things to jump over, crawl under, climb over, and go around. It's like a race, but with all sorts of challenges along the way to make it interesting and fun.

Hide Under Your Bed

Do you fit? What's under there? Who can you spy on? Does anyone know where you are? Call someone and see if they can find you. See if you can get them to hide with you. Can you get the whole family under there?

Note to kids: If your parents read this to you, then they are going to be onto the whole hide under the bed and call them trick. But if you wait a few days, they'll probably forget about this little trick (adults are forgetful that way) and come looking for you and wonder where you could possibly be. Tuck this idea away for later.

Note to parents: Play along if your kids try this trick on you. They can't wait to try out tricks and probably won't be able to wait until you have truly forgotten about this one.

Juggle

Juggling can be tricky, but it is so much fun and really impresses people when you can do it. I mean, *really* impresses people. At least people worth impressing.

Start by gently tossing one ball from one hand to the other. Toss the ball so it goes about as high as your head, maybe a little higher. Keep doing this until you can throw it from hand to hand without looking at the ball and without having to move your feet around to catch the ball. Be patient; this is the slowest and most boring part of learning to juggle and it takes awhile. But mastering this will make the rest way easier.

Once you have that working well, you can start juggling two balls. Start with one ball in each hand. Toss one ball from one hand to the other. Just before it is going to land, toss the other ball to the other hand so you have an empty hand to catch the first ball. Be prepared to spend a lot of time picking up balls. Once you are able to juggle two balls (you're juggling!!!!), add in a third.

Once you can juggle balls, what else can you try? Scarves? Oranges? Whatever you decide to juggle, I don't recommend eggs!

Tip: The best juggling balls are little bean bags, or small, same-sized, slightly squishy balls that fit nicely in the palm of your hand. Tennis balls seem like a great idea, but they're a bit big—especially for kids.

Peaksay Igpay Atinlay (Speak Pig Latin)

Pig Latin is strange but fun. Take the first letter of a word and put it on the end of the word, then add 'ay' to the end.

Examples (To help you out the **bolded** letter is the first letter of the word in its new spot. The *italicized* letters are the 'ay' added onto the end):

Hello: ello**H***ay*
My **n**ame **i**s: y**M***ay* amen*ay* si*ay*
Bike: ike**B***ay*

Tip: Your grandparents will probably think you're pretty cool if you can speak to them in Pig Latin.

Dizzy Spin

Spin until you are dizzy. Are you dizzy yet? How about now? No? Keep spinning!

Okay, now try walking in a straight line. Can you do it? How far can you get? How much do you have to spin until you're dizzy? Can you still touch your nose? Can you hop without falling over?

Gymnastics

Try cartwheels, somersaults, handstands, and more! Make a whole routine with your friends to show off to your family.

Martial Arts

Karate, Kung Fu, Tai Kwon Do, Judo, and Jujitsu are several forms of martial arts. If you don't know any "real" moves, make up your own.

Jump on Your Bed

(If you're allowed. If you're not, well, I'm sorry I brought it up. And if you are allowed, don't be like the monkeys in the song and fall off and bump your head, okay? Be careful!)

Half Finger

Point your index fingers together about an inch apart and about two inches away from your face. Stare at the space between your fingers and beyond. You should see a weird half finger between your real fingers! Don't see it? Move your fingers around until you find the 'sweet' spot.

Yo-Yo Tricks
Do you know any yo-yo tricks? Here's one to get you started…

Around the World:
Make sure you have lots of room around and above you for this trick so you don't bean someone in the nose. To make your yo-yo go "around the world," wait until the yo-yo reaches the end of its string when letting it out, then instead of jerking the string to return the yo-yo to your hand, use your wrist to swing the yo-yo up and around in a big circle that goes up over your yo-yo shoulder. (Try to keep your hand in one spot while the yo-yo swings around.) Once the yo-yo comes back down behind you and around to your feet, jerk the string to bring the yo-yo back up to your hand. Don't worry if you don't get it the first time—it takes timing and practice.

Do you know any other yo-yo tricks? Can you make up your own?

Tip: Solid wood yo-yos work the best as they have the weight to come back up to your hand nicely and usually have a good string on them, too. Once you have the hang of getting your yo-yo to return to your hand after releasing it, try tricks like Around the World.

Practical Jokes
Make sure your joke won't hurt anyone because then it wouldn't be funny, just mean.

Short Sheeting Someone's Bed
To short sheet someone's bed, take the blanket, pillow and top (flat) sheet off the bed. Now, take the top (flat) sheet and tuck the bottom end of it under the head-end of the mattress where you would normally place the pillow. Now smooth the sheet down over the bed. About halfway down, fold the loose end of the sheet back up towards the head end of the bed where the other end is tucked in. Place the blanket over the sheet like you were making the bed, then fold the extra end of the top sheet over the edge of the blanket so it looks normal.

But… when someone tries to slide their feet down into their made bed, they won't be able to because their sheet is folded or "short sheeted." Tee hee.

Tip: If you have a fake dog poop or a fake spider, place that in there to give them an extra fun scare as well!

Palm Reading
Can you read someone's future by looking at the lines on their palms?

Stunt double...
Safety first: Start with small tricks and work your way up. Always wear protective gear and ask for adult help and advice BEFORE trying any and all stunts. Always, always.
- Bicycle wheelies
- Jumps and spins on your skateboard
- Scooter tricks
- In-line skating squats, spins, and more!

Shoot Elastic Bands

Ceiling Stars
To make stars on your ceiling, you will need a dark room, flashlight, and a strainer or colander.

Simply turn out the lights and shine the flashlight up through the strainer. Ta-da! Stars on your ceiling.

Want to take your stars to the next level? Punch tiny holes (a sharpened pencil works well for this) in the surface of a cardboard box. You can punch the holes in the shapes of constellations or shapes like flowers or rockets or even write words or messages.

Phoon
Take a photo of yourself phooning somewhere odd and unusual. What's a phoon pose? Running man side profile. Yup, that crazy simple. Or just crazy. Stand sideways to the camera on one leg, the other out behind you like your mid-run. One arm bent and in front of you, one behind you.

Create a Secret Handshake

Whose Got Your Nose?
A fun one for toddlers!

Pretend to pinch off the other person's nose and as you do so, stick the tip of your thumb between your index and pointer finger as proof that you have their nose. (Your thumb sort of looks like a nose when it's peeking out between your fingers.)

Make Goofy Insults
My kids love this one. Nothing mean, nothing personal, just pure silliness.

Some family favorites that get the kids rolling on the floor laughing (they like to build off each other's insults):

Your butt smells like ducks in the bathroom sink!
Your butt smells like rainbow barf.
 The sillier the better. Betcha laugh!

Note: If a player starts to get upset, it's probably time to stop. This game is meant to be good fun for everyone and not something that will hurt the feelings of others. While the game helps teach kids how to let things roll off their backs and how not to take teasing personally, it can sometimes start to feel like too much.

Monkeys Always Look!
Point to something and say, "Look!" I bet your friend looks! When they do, say, "Monkeys always look!" Be ready! If they know this one they might reply, "Apes always tell them to!"

In my family this game has skipped the monkeys and evolved into: "Is that a chicken!" (Say it as you point.)

Scratch Inside Your Head
Bend your pointer finger and stick the knuckle in your right ear. Then, stick your tongue into your cheek on the left side of your head. As you 'scratch,' tilt your hand up and down while moving your tongue in unison so it looks as though your tongue is actually the end of your finger scratching inside your head! Practice this one in front of the mirror to get the timing right.

Wet Willies
In case you didn't have enough ways to torture your sibling...

These are kind of... gross. Wet your finger and stick it in someone's ear. They're guaranteed to hate it.

Guess What?

"Mom, guess what?"

"What?"

"Mom, guess what?"

"What?"

"Mom, guess what?" (She's feeling a tad impatient with you by now… you'll have to judge how far you can push this one. Maybe repeat the question only twice. Maybe more. Maybe mix it up by saying it differently each time… you get the picture.)

"What?"

"I forgot."

<Groan>

Hint: You can play this one with anyone. It doesn't have to be poor ol' Mom.

Take the Elevator/Escalator/Stairs

This gag needs a good prop where you can hide your lower body behind it. For example, a couch or half wall. Stand on one side of the couch or half wall with your audience on the other. Say something witty such as, "I forgot something on the first floor. I guess I need to take the elevator." Or, "Let's ride the escalator to the toy department!" Or, "I need to go downstairs to get my homework." (I'm sure you can come up with something wittier than that but you get the idea.) Then…

If in an 'elevator'… turn to the side and push an imaginary button to take you down to the first floor. Then, slowly bend your knees so you look like you're taking an elevator down through the floor as you sink behind your prop.

If on an 'escalator'… climb aboard and slowing bend your knees and sink down smoothly while stepping forward so it looks like an escalator is taking you down!

If taking the 'stairs'… take a step forward at the same time as sinking down so it looks like you are stepping down steps. This one is tricky—it might take some practice to make it look right.

Move Objects with Your Mind

Can you move that pencil on the desk just by thinking about it? Concentrate now…

Whoa! Did it just move? Try it again.

Swallowing Noodle Trick

This is not for everyone… Trust me. I can't believe I'm going to share this one with you as I've grossed A LOT of people out doing this trick. All you need is one long, cooked spaghetti noodle and the willingness to be completely gross.

Ready? Hold one end of the noodle, then put the rest in your mouth and swallow it while still holding onto the one end. Swallowed? Here's the disgusting part. Pull the swallowed part of the noodle back out!

Ugh. I can't believe I thought that was a cool trick when I was a teenager. Although, seeing the grossed out look on boys' faces made it all worth it.

Swinging Water Bucket

Can you swing a bucket (with 1 cup of water in it) around upside down without spilling its water?

Hint: Swing the bucket up and around and down very quickly (making a large circle with your arm). Centrifugal force will hold the water in the bucket. Watch out for your legs when the bucket comes down again as it is easy to smack them. Ouch!

P.S. Don't try this one inside. (Just in case…)

Keep a Balloon in the Air

Try to keep it from touching the ground. How many times (or for how long) can you bump it (no catching!) before you miss and it hits the floor?

Pop Balloons by Sitting on Them

Crazy Flying Balloon

Blow up a balloon, but don't tie it closed. Instead, let go of the balloon and watch it fly all crazy as the air zips out. It makes such a weird noise too!

Squealing Balloons

Blow up a balloon, but don't tie it closed. Using both hands, pinch the stem of the balloon (where you blow into) and stretch it so air can't escape. Relax the stem enough that air slowly leaks out. When you get it right, it will make a loud squealing noise that will freak out the cats.

Balloon Animals
You will need: long, thin balloons made especially for balloon animals.

What animals can you make by twisting the balloon? Can you add balloons to other balloons to make an even bigger animal?

Static Balloons
Rub a balloon in your hair and then stick the balloon to the wall. If enough static electricity has been built up between your hair and the balloon, the balloon will stick to the wall. It should make your hair nice and crazy too!

Levitating Balloons
Hold your balloon over a floor vent—furnace or air-conditioning—while it is running and see if the air coming out of the vent will make your balloon levitate. (That means float.)

MAD SCIENTIST'S OOEY GOOEY LABRATORY

Children are driven to explore their world because new discoveries bring them joy.

Gabrielle Principe, Your Brain on Childhood

Rats exposed to play experienced great amounts of brain growth whereas rats who were not exposed to play did not experience nearly the brain growth. Play is an activity that helps grow kid brains too! As well, play is a way for kids to learn in an environment that is nonthreatening to their physical or emotional well-being. So let's get down to it!

Crystals _Safety First:_ Have an adult boil and pour the water for this activity.

Crystals are a scientific mystery. Okay, not really. Scientists say crystals are an organized group of atoms and molecules. Personally, I say they're just really cool to make, look at, and touch. What do you think?

Let's try it.

To make your own crystals, you will need:
¼ cup (60 mL) of table salt
¾ cup (180 mL) water
a pot, spoon, measuring cup, saucer, and a piece of paper big enough to cover the top of the saucer.

With help from an adult, bring the water to a boil. Remove from heat. Slowly stir the salt into the water, a little bit at a time. The water may be cloudy from the salt, but keep adding salt until it no longer dissolves (it starts to stay on the bottom of the pot after a lot of stirring and doesn't mix into the water and disappear). Have an adult pour the hot, salty water into a saucer. (If there are bits of salt at the bottom of the pot, don't pour it into the saucer. Any extra salty water can be poured down the drain. Make sure you rinse the sink as all that salt can be hard on your sink's surface.)

Cover the saucer with a piece of paper. Let the saucer sit (**don't move it at all**) for the next few days while the water _slowly_ evaporates. You should see crystals start to form within a few days to a week.

What size and shape are they? Do you have a magnifying glass or microscope? Take a closer peek!

Tip: You can also make crystals by substituting sugar instead of salt. Do the sugar crystals look different? Why or why not?

Painted Flowers
Change the color of a white flower with the magic of osmosis and other fancy science terms.

It's this simple. Place a white flower such as a daisy in a glass with food coloring, and watch its petals change color over a day or two as it drinks up the colored water.

Capillary Flower

You will need: A square piece of paper, scissors, a sink or tub of water.

Using your scissors, cut a flower shape out of paper. Then cut four petals toward the flower's center so you can fold them in separately. When you fold the petals in, fold them over the center so you have a 'closed' flower—really, the petals are just all folded in on top of each other.

Lay your paper flower in a sink or tub of water, letting it float on the water's surface. Capillary action will cause the paper to draw in water. This will unfold your flower, opening it.

Echo… Echo… Echo

Sound bounces best off of bare areas with hard objects, like a large rock wall, creating an echo. (The sound keeps bouncing around so we hear it more than once.) At home, you can make an echo in a bare bathroom (remove towels hanging off towel racks or other soft objects from the bathroom as they can 'suck up' the sound so you can't make an echo).

Fingerprints

Everyone's fingerprints are different. Want to get a good look at yours? Take a pencil and color a dark splotch on a piece of paper. Then rub your finger in the splotch until you have all that pencil stuff on your finger's print. Then place your dirty finger on a piece of clear tape. The tape will pull off an imprint of your fingerprint. Stick the tape to a clean, white piece of paper and take a good look at the swirls, lakes, and ridges of your fingerprint. Are all of your fingers the same? Or are they different?

Freeze Frame Video

Take photos of your toy car moving slowly across your camera frame or a doll walking. Each photo is just a tiny movement each. Then put them all together in a movie. Can you do it? It's tricky and take a lot of patience and attention to small details.

Look Through a Magnifying Glass

A magnifying glass makes things look bigger, and often you can see things that you wouldn't be able to see with just your eyes. What should you look at? Your toys? Leaves? Grass? Insects? Words in a book? Your own eye in the mirror?

Far Becomes Near: Binoculars

Safety First: Never look at the sun (with or without binoculars) as it can damage your eyes permanently.

What do you see through the binoculars? Does it look different? What have you always wanted to see, but it was too far away? Now's your chance! What happens if you look through the other end of the binoculars?

What's Hotter?

Place different colored pieces of paper in the window/sun (black, white, color) and try to guess which one will get hotter. (Explain why some colors get hotter—absorb rays instead of reflect.)

Yucky Concoctions

Have to do the dishes? Combine all the weird bits that are left over in a glass. How yucky can you make it? What about those bits of mashed potato? Coffee? Milk? Bacon fat? Stir it up! Ewwwwww!

Volcano

You will need:

1 cup (250 mL) vinegar

4 tbsp (60 mL) baking soda

4 drops red food coloring (optional)

6 drops dish detergent

1 stir stick that reaches the bottom of your volcano (a long straw works nicely)

1 jar or bottle (This will be your volcano. You can also make a volcano from clay or paper maché (find the recipes for clay and paper maché in the Construction Crafts section). For now, let's keep it simple—a bottle will do fine.)

In your jar or bottle, dump in your baking soda, food coloring, and dish detergent. Pour in the vinegar and give it a slight stir. You should get a bubbly eruption! It's THAT easy!

Got Toddlers? Try this—place your volcano in the middle of the kitchen sink or basin with an inch or so of water in the bottom. Give the kiddos some toy boats or other toys and let the volcano erupt!

Glop

You will need:

½ cup (125 mL) milk

¼ cup (60 mL) vinegar

measuring cup

coffee filter or paper towel

Warm milk to room temperature using a microwave. Add vinegar. Stir. Bubbles and small lumps will start to form. Strain the liquid by pouring it through a coffee filter or paper towel. What is left in the filter is your glop. Isn't it all ooey and gooey? Talk about weird!

Flubber

You will need:

2 tsp (10 mL) Borax

1 cup (250 mL) warm water

white glue

container such as an ice cream pail

Add the Borax to warm water. Add white glue. Stir well. Let it sit for a minute. Mix it again with your hands. The glue becomes Flubber, so the more glue you add, the more Flubber you will make. Really mix the glue well, otherwise you will have gluey areas in your Flubber.

Hint: If you want to make a ball, form it when you take the Flubber out of the water. As the Flubber dries out, it becomes more firm and harder to shape. It's bouncy!

Silly Putty

You will need:

2 cups (500 mL) white glue

1 cup (250 mL) liquid starch

bowl or pail

Mix the glue and starch together using your hands. Once it has formed a ball, knead it with your hands for 5-10 minutes. If it is too sticky, add more starch. If it is too runny, add more glue. Have fun!

Glump

You will need:

1 cup (250 mL) cornstarch
½ cup (125 mL) water
bowl (a glass or metal bowl works better than a soft flexible bowl)
food coloring (optional)

Place cornstarch in a bowl and add a little bit of water at a time. The Glump isn't going to seem very gooey. In fact, it is going to be quite hard and difficult to stir. Stir until there is no more dry cornstarch, but don't add too much water! Keep adding water and stirring and testing to see if the Glump drips from a spoon. When it drips off a spoon, it is ready.

Now what? Play! Talk about sensory!

Playdough

You will need help from an adult and these ingredients:

2 cups (500 mL) flour
2 cups (500 mL) water
1 cup (250 mL) salt
2 tbsp (30 mL) oil
4 tbsp (60 mL) cream of tartar
food coloring (if you want to make different colored playdough)

Combine the above ingredients in a pot, and ask an adult to cook the mixture on the stove over medium heat. Heat until the dough starts to leave the side of the pot. Cook for a few minutes more. (Don't overcook or you playdough will get kind of hard.) Let it cool. Once cool, knead the playdough until smooth. It's now ready for an adventure!

Hint: After playing with your playdough, store it in a sealed bag. It will last a long time and is way better than the store bought stuff.

Pick Your Nose

So… how bored are you exactly? Bored enough to pick your nose? If so, remember this rule of thumb (or finger): You can pick your friends, and you can pick your nose, but you can't pick your friend's nose.

Wiggle Your Toes in Cold Noodles or Jell-O

Extra sensory! Can you handle the squish?

Sidewalk Chalk Recipe
You will need:
1 cup (250 mL) water
1 cup (250 mL) Plaster of Paris
powdered tempra paint
molds (empty toilet paper rolls with the end sealed with aluminum foil or cling wrap)
spoon
bowl

Mix water and plaster as per the plaster's instructions. Mix in paint powder for color. (To make swirly colored chalk, use two or three different colors and mix them together just slightly.) Let the colored mixture sit for one minute before pouring it into your molds.

Set your molds aside until they are completely dry. Remove your chalk from the molds and let them dry even longer (about 24 hours). The bigger your molds, the longer it will take for your chalk to dry all the way through to the middle.

Have a Spitting Contest
Go outside (please!) and see who can spit the farthest.

Spitballs
This is a gross one that can get you in trouble because you're going to be spitting gross gobs. Consider yourself warned! (And don't do this one in the house, okay? Ew.)

Take a small piece of paper or paper towel and chew it up in your mouth until it's a moist ball. (Told you it was gross.) Now spit it! What can you get it to stick to?

Want to make a pea shooter? Take a wide straw or a pen (take the inside guts out of the pen so you have a firm plastic straw). Place your spitball in one end and blow out the other end, sending your spitball flying.

FOOD FUN

Play is preparation for life.

David Elkind, The Hurried Child

Who says you can't have fun with your food? A chapter of recipes, goofy challenges, and more.

Spider Dogs
It's a wiener roast… only cooler!

Safety First: Ask an adult to cut "legs" into your wiener. On each end, slice an "X," cutting the X almost down to the middle of the wiener. Do the same on the other end, but don't let the legs on one end reach the legs on the other end. You should have 4 "legs" on each end, making a total of 8 legs. Stick your wiener on your roasting stick and as it cooks, the legs will curl up a little bit making it look like a spider.

Hint: You can make these on the BBQ, too.

Toast Marshmallows
To toast marshmallows, let your fire burn down to just coals or very small flames.

Place a marshmallow on a roasting stick and hold it over the coals.

Safety First: Your fire will still be very hot. As well, marshmallows catch on fire quite easily and burn very hot when they do. If your marshmallow catches on fire, *slowly* remove it from the fire as toasted marshmallows can get very slippery on their stick and you don't want to be winging a flaming marshmallow at someone by accident.

S'mores
You don't always need a campfire to make these yummy treats. Try this at-home microwave method.

Ingredients: arrowroot cookies, graham crackers or chocolate coated biscuits, and chocolate chips or pieces of chocolate bar, and marshmallows.

Put a cookie or cracker on a plate and place your chocolate on top. Place a marshmallow on top of the chocolate. Heat in the microwave for a few seconds until the marshmallow starts to get puffy. Take it out of the microwave and add another cracker or cookie on top. Push down lightly. Let it cool and enjoy.

Safety First: Careful! They can be very hot.

Campfire Method: Roast a marshmallow over the campfire coals, place it on a cookie with chocolate, add another cookie over top, smash it all together and enjoy!

Bannock/Fry Bread

Bannock is a traditional Native American recipe. There are many different recipes for Bannock. Ask an adult to help you use the oven.

Ingredients:
4-5 cups (1L – 1250 mL) white flour
¼ lb (125 g) lard
3 tbsp (45 mL) baking powder
2 ½ cups (625 mL) water **or** milk
1 tsp (5 mL) salt

Mix flour, salt, and baking powder in a bowl. Mix in the lard with your hands until the mix is crumbly. Then add milk/water. Grease a 9 x 13 inch (23 x 33 cm) pan. Knead the dough down in the pan until it covers the bottom of the pan. Bake at 350 F (175 C) for 30-40 minutes.

Hint: Bannock tastes *great* warm with butter and jam. You can also cook it over a campfire by wrapping a thin layer of dough over a stick.

Slurp your Noodles

How much noise can you make while eating? Drinking?

Hint: Grab a straw for maximum drink slurp.

Eat by Candlelight

Safety First: Be sure to let an adult light the candle, and never leave a candle unattended.

Drink Bubbles

Can you blow bubbles in your drink? Use a straw and see if you can blow enough bubbles your drink *almost* overflows.

Eat Something New

Is there a food you always wanted to try, but haven't? Buy it! Bake it! Cook it!

Have a Food Fight

Spoons make excellent launchers for peas. Just don't throw anything you don't want to clean up later!

More...
- Eat with Chopsticks
- Laugh Until Milk Comes Out Your Nose
- Make a Meal for Your Parents
- Cook an Entire Meal Over a Fire

Suck Food Through Your Teeth
Recently lost a tooth? Even better! Suck Jell-O, pudding, or soup through your teeth and that new hole where a tooth used to be. What else is good to suck through your teeth?

Colored Celery
Place a stick of celery in a glass of water that contains food coloring. As the piece of celery sucks up the colored water, you will notice the 'veins' inside of the celery stem turns that color. Cool!

Super-Easy Ice-Cream
To make one serving you will need to mix together in a small zip top bag:
½ cup (125 mL) half-and-half cream
¼ tsp (1 mL) vanilla
1 tbsp (15 mL) white granulated sugar

Press air out of the bag and seal it.

Mix together in a large zip top bag:
ice (enough to half fill a large zip top bag)
2 tbsp (30 mL) coarse salt

Stir the salt so it coats the ice. Then put the small bag in the big bag. Squeeze the air out of the large bag and seal it. Jiggle, squeeze and toss the bag for 10 minutes. Brrrrr... you might need your winter gloves as you and a friend toss this around.

Ta-da! Soft ice-cream!

Hint: Want more flavors? Try adding crushed peppermint candies (or candy canes), chopped and drained frozen fruit, chocolate... What else?

Smoothie

A smoothie is a thick drink made with lots of fruit.

There are many different smoothie recipes. You can use all sorts of different fruits—frozen or fresh. Frozen fruits will make your smoothie thicker—as will bananas. You can add milk or soy milk as a base for your smoothie so it's not super crazy thick. There is no need to add sugar. Just throw everything in a blender or hand mixer—*get help from an adult*—and mix it all until the fruit is smooth.

Milkshake

Mix ice cream or frozen yogurt in a blender along with frozen or fresh fruit. You may have to add a little bit of milk or soy milk to make it less thick.

Hint: Bananas will help make it thicker.

Sundae

Scoop ice cream into a bowl and add yummy toppings like chocolate chips, chocolate sauce, strawberries, bananas, sprinkles, nuts, peanut butter, and pancake syrup/ice cream syrup to create a marvelous sundae.

Frozen Juice Popsicles

If you don't have popsicle molds, you can use ice cube trays to make mini popsicles using toothpicks for sticks.

Pour your chosen juice into your container and freeze for a few hours. Voila! Juice-icles!

Colored Ice-Cubes

Add food coloring to the water you pour into your ice cube tray to make fun ice cubes. If you have small plastic insects or dinosaurs, add those in for a fun surprise.

Bake Cookies

What kind of cookies would you like to bake today? What's your favorite recipe? If the adults in your life are unable to help with the oven right now, do you have a no-bake recipe you can make?

Guess the Color

While someone feeds you food while blindfolded, try to guess what color the food is. Some foods might be easy… so might be more difficult.

Peanut Butter Balls
Ingredients:
1 cup (250 mL) peanut butter
2/3 cup (80 mL) powdered milk
¼ cup (60 mL) coconut
½ cup (125 mL) raisins
¼ cup (60 mL) honey

Mix all ingredients together. Make small balls or other shapes and enjoy!

Hint: These treats freeze well for an easy on-hand treat.

Homemade Dog Treats
There are all TONS of homemade dog treat recipes online. Find a recipe that looks like your cup of tea and give it a go. Your dog will love them! (And they'll love you too!)

Hint: Search for "homemade dog treats," "dog treat recipes," or "dog biscuit recipes."

Have a Picnic
Is it yucky outside? Bring the picnic inside! Our family has an indoor picnic blanket for when we picnic inside—we do it that often! Sometimes it's a picnic and a movie 'date' the whole family goes on in the living room.

Mini-Pizzas
Crust ideas: Make your own from scratch or use mini-pitas (found in the bread aisle) or pre-made crusts.

Sauce ideas: Use canned pizza sauce, salsa, alfredo sauce, or olive oil mixed with Parmesan and garlic.

Toppings: Be creative! Cheese, olives, peppers, pineapple, mushrooms, cooked chicken, salami, pepperoni, canned tuna, ground beef, cooked potato, sausage, broccoli, tomatoes, mushrooms, cooked noodles...

Have an adult pop your pizzas in the oven at 350F (175 C) or toaster oven until the cheese turns light brown around the edges.

Eat In a New To You Restaurant

Peel an Apple or Orange in One Piece
Safety First: The apple challenge is ONLY for older kids who are allowed to use knives sharp enough for peeling.

Feeling left out? No worries. Grab an orange and see if you can peel it in one big piece. Mandarin/Christmas oranges are especially awesome for being able to do this without breaking the peel into pieces. Can you make elephant ears and a trunk with the peel? What else? A snake?

Play With Your Food
That's right! Play! You know what to do. Use your fingers. Make a forest with your broccoli. Make faces with your veggie slices. Stick carrots up your nose... no, wait. Don't do that last one.

Cookies in a Jar
This makes a great gift.

You'll need a large jar. Then layer in, one at a time for a really neat effect:
3/4 cup (190 mL) white flour
3/4 cup (190 mL) brown sugar
1/4 cup (60 mL) white sugar
1/4 tsp (1 mL) baking soda
1/4 tsp (1 mL) baking powder
1/2 cup (125 mL) raisins
1/2 cup (125 mL) rolled oats
3/4 cup (190 mL) chocolate chips

You will need to write up a tag to go with the cookie jar that includes these instructions:

Preheat oven to 375 F (190 C).

In addition to the jar's ingredients you will need:
6 tbsp (90 mL) butter
1 tsp (5 mL) vanilla
1 egg

In a large bowl, mix the egg, butter, and vanilla, then add the contents from the jar and stir until your cookie dough is smooth. Bake on a cookie sheet for 8 minutes.

Guess the Food
Have someone feed you food while you are blindfolded. Try to guess what they fed you.

Apple Mouth
Take two apple slices and spread peanut butter on one side of each slice. Place mini marshmallows along one of the apple and peanut butter wedges. These will be the mouth's teeth. Place the other apple slice on top to make the mouth's top lip. Ta-da! A mouth that you can eat.

Hint: You can substitute the peanut butter for pea butter.

Food Mouth
You could also call this activity Orange Mouth. Or Cucumber Teeth. Or even Carrot Fangs.

Know what time it is? Time to play with your food again! Yes!

Take an orange wedge and pop it in your mouth. Doesn't the peel look like orange teeth? What about a long slice of cucumber? If you eat the white part, leaving the peel, can you wrap the peel around your teeth to make green teeth? How about a tomato wedge? (Lovely red lips, you have my dear.) And carrot sticks. Oh, carrot sticks! They make such *lovely* fangs.

What else do you have on your plate? Let's see what we can do with that, too.

Food Sculptures
I think it's time to build something yummy on your plate. What do you think? Could we make a car? House? Rabbit? Let's try it!

You're going to need some glue. How about peanut butter, cream cheese, pea butter? Excellent. We're also going to need some building supplies like crackers—they make excellent walls for a house, don't you think? And that car will need wheels... have any round snacks in the cupboard? Stick it all together with your 'glue' and see what happens.

Watermelon Seed Spitting Contest
It might be tricky finding a watermelon with seeds, but if you can find one, see who can spit them the farthest (outside) or the most at one time.

Banana Message

Want to send someone a secret message, and all you have are a banana and a pencil? No problem! Press the pencil (or other slightly sharpish object) into the peel's skin so it dents it, but isn't super noticeable. Write your message, then in a few hours the message should appear as the 'bruise' in the peel develops. (Your message's letters will look black.)

Bobbing for Mini Donuts

This is just like bobbing for apples except there are no apples and no water. Otherwise, as my friend Leslie used to say, "Exactly the same only different."

Tie mini donuts on strings and hang them where the kids can try to bite them off and eat them! No hands allowed to help you out! How much do you want that donut? Get in there!

LET'S PRETEND: IMAGINARY PLAY

When children engage in imaginary play they can be anyone, anywhere, and at any time. Children put a lot of back-end cultural and societal understanding and problem-solving in one play session involving a pretend world. What's feasible? What's not? And if that's not feasible and I want it to be, how must this imaginary world change in order to accommodate that?

But it's more than just that, according to the authors of *Einstein Never Used Flashcards*. When children engage in imaginary play it leads to an essential intellectual and social advantage as they learn to cope with not only a myriad of feelings while breaking their big, confusing world down into a manageable size, but they also learn how to become socially adept as they share, put themselves into the shoes of others, and practice being flexible while taking turns and making concessions during cooperational play.

Does imaginary play still sound a bit dreamy and abstract? Well, they also say pretend play allows for symbol manipulation which is a platform for symbolic thinking in language, math, physics, economics, art, and literature. While that is some pretty fancy language, I think we get the point. Imaginative play is an important foundation for further future learning and helps set young brains up for the skills they'll need later in life. And *that* sounds pretty good, doesn't it?

So, put on your fairy wings, it's time to play…

Pretend You're a Grown Up
What are adults like? Do they sit around and talk about broccoli and mortgages all day? Or do they do other things? What about their jobs? What do you want to be when you grow up? Pretend you're already grown up and going to that job.

Pretend You're an Animal
What animal are you? What does it eat? How does it move? Where does it live? What sounds does it make?

Pretend You're Blind
Close your eyes (or blindfold yourself) and walk around. What's it like? Is it easier than you thought it would be? Is it scary? Comforting? Can you hear more things when you are relying on your other senses? What do you notice?

Safety First: Make sure you play this game in a safe place (for example, away from hot stoves, stairs, and breakable objects). As well, to help keep you safe, have a friend be your guide and allow them to give you directions. Follow their directions and see where they lead you. (Did you end up where you thought you were going? Or did you get turned around and all mixed up?) Take turns being blind.

Boy/Girl
Are you a girl? Pretend you're a boy. What do they talk like? Walk like? Act like?
Are you a boy? Pretend you're a girl. What do they talk like? Walk like? Act like?

Someone You Know
Pretend to be someone you know. What do they talk like? How do they dress? How do they treat others?

Bumper Cars
Walk and spin around letting yourself bump into things and your friends just like you were a bumper car.

Safety First: Be gentle. Before you start, move anything breakable or sharp out of the way so you don't bump into it. In fact, you might want to play this one outdoors where you have plenty of space.

Spend a Million Bucks ($1,000,000)
I loved this one as a kid—it was harder to spend a million than I thought it would be.

Grab a piece of paper and a calculator. Look through catalogues and flyers to help you make a list of things you want to pretend-buy with your million dollars. Can you spend it all?

Hmmm… I wonder how much a swimming pool would cost?

Create an Invisible Friend
What's their favorite food? Their name? Do they only show up when you're bored, when there is ice-cream, or when your brother is bugging you?

Pretend You're a Spy
It's secret mission time!

Need help decking yourself out in a spy game? Fear not! Check out these other activities and learn how to make your own secret code (found in the Kids Stuff section), do some invisible writing (found in Literary Play), create your spy headquarters (a fort), tin can phones (found in the Construction Crafts section), create your own spyglass or binoculars (found in Artistic Play) as well as a periscope (found in the Construction Crafts section).

Mime
Mimes can't talk or make noises. They act out what they are thinking or want to say by using their hands, body and facial expressions. Give it a whirl. Do you like it? Is it tricky?

Pretend you are...

- Famous
- Invisible
- A Snake or a Slug
- A Superhero
- An Alien
- An Airplane
- Exploring a Foreign Land
- On a Magic Carpet
- A Princess/Prince
- A Character from a Book
- Flying

KIDS STUFF: JUST PLAY

Children who indulge themselves regularly in play tend to have advanced language abilities, display more creative thinking, exhibit better memory, and show better problem-solving skills. They also tend to be less stressed and have strong social skills.

Gabrielle Principe
Your Brain on Childhood

Children are at their *highest* level of development when they are at play. It may look as though your child is wasting time and learning nothing, but according to David Elkind (author of *The Power of Play*) "it is vitally important to support and encourage self-directed activity… Even if those activities appear meaningless to us, they can have great purpose and significance for the child. These acts are not random and have a pattern and organization in keeping with the child's level of mental ability. Allowing children time and freedom to complete these activities to her personal satisfaction nurses that child's powers of concentration and attention." Further, "We run the risk of impairing the powers if we don't respect and value the young child's self-initiated activity." He continues to say that self-initiated play can be very complex in terms of social rules and socialization. As well, children are learning important, intricate skills on how to be an effective social being while playing.

In other words, we, as parents and caregivers, need to teach ourselves to trust our child's play priorities and allow them the space and freedom to follow their passions and pleasures—just like we'd like to do, too.

P.S. Did you know that complex block play is linked to the development of math skills?

Tea Party
Who wants tea? (Imaginary, real, or simply juice in toy teacups.) Friends are all busy? Have a tea party with your dolls or teddy bears.

Blow Bubbles
If you don't have bubble making solution or a wand, you can make your own using the recipe below.

Make Your Own Bubble Solution
You will need:
small container (deeper is better than wider)
2 tsp (10 mL) dish soap (Joy™ and Dawn™ work well)
¼ cup (60 mL) water
5 mL (1 tsp) glycerin (Optional. Glycerin makes bubbles stronger. *Hint:* You can find glycerin in most drug stores.)

Mix all ingredients together in the container.

Hint: The bubble mix is better the second day, so if you have the time, make it the day before.

Bubble Bottle
This is a fun toddler toy. Fill a small plastic bottle with water and dish soap. Add glitter, yarn, food coloring, or other interesting things if you want more than just bubbles. Test out your shaker before you glue the lid on.

Make Your Own Bubble Wand
To make your own bubble wand, take a thin piece of wire. Bend one end into a small loop (a circle). Dip into the bubble mixture (recipe above). Want your wand to hold more bubble solution? Wrap yarn around the loop.

Other bubble wand ideas: fly swatter, a hole cut in a plastic lid from a yogurt container, your hands—make a circle with your thumb and pointer finger. What else can you use to form bubbles?

Build...
- A Block Tower
- A City Out of Blocks
- Something with Lego (or other inter-locking blocks)
- Tape Roads (*Hint:* Use painter's tape—it comes off easily, doesn't wreck most furniture and doesn't leave sticky residue—to make roads over the floor and furniture)
- Something Massive or Super Cool (Dig through the family's recycle bin. Milk carton castle anyone?)

Jump Rope
Long rope or short rope? One player or three?

One rope, one person? Easy! Skip away. See how many times you can jump without tripping up the rope.

Long rope, three people? Awesome! Get out the jump rope songs and challenges! Don't know any? Your parents might or you can look some up online or even make your own.

Hint: Have two short ropes, but want a long one? Tie two short ropes together.

Join a Club
There are clubs for just about everything! What are you interested in? What do you like?

Shadow Figures/Shadow Puppets

Shine a light against a wall in a dark room. Hold your hands up between the light and the wall and make different shadow shapes. Can you make rabbit ears? How about other animals?

Leap Frog

Players crouch into a ball on the ground all in a line. The player at the back of the line is the leap frog and leaps over the other frogs by placing a leg on either side of the crouched frog while placing their hands on the crouched frog's back. They then push off with their hands and leap, landing in front of the crouched frog. Once they reach the front of the line, they crouch down, becoming one of the frogs to leap over and the new back-of-the-line player is now the leap frog.

Play...
- With a Friend or Sibling
- Dress-up
- House
- School
- With Action Figures or Dolls

Cars

Make roads and cities (and ramps!) for your cars and trucks out of blocks or paper, cardboard boxes, painter's tape on the floor and furniture… be creative!

Playdough

Want to take your playdough play time up a level? Bring on the dinosaurs! Bring on the cars! Bring on… whatever you want to get dirty in the playdough.

Hint: Need a recipe? Find one in the Mad Scientist's Ooey Gooey Laboratory section.

Video Games

Are you tired of your games? Borrow a friend's or ask your parents if you can trade some in.

Play in a Tent

Don't have to have a real tent? Make one out of a blanket and a rope. Tie the rope between two trees or two chairs and drape your blanket over the rope. Pull the sides of the blanket out and crawl in.

Globe Trotter

Where will you live when you grow up? Got a globe? Spin it, then lightly drag your finger along its surface as it spins. When it stops spinning, wherever your finger lands is the place where you will live when you grow up! (Do you think it's true?)

Start a Collection

What would you like to collect? Stamps? Bottle caps? Sticks? Buttons? Stickers? Sports cards? Find something interesting and start collecting. Maybe you already have a collection? Take it out, look at it and reorganize it. Do you have two of something in your collection? Trade with a friend!

Invent a New Career

What job do you figure hasn't been invented yet? A professional tree climber? Maybe a video game tester (those actually exist). Maybe a bird whistle imitator? What would this new career look like? What would you do? Feel free to be silly!

Plan a Perfect Dream Day

What would your perfect day look like? Would someone bring you French toast in bed? Would you spend all day at the swimming pool? Would your brother or sister have to be your servant?

Plan a Perfect Dream Trip or Vacation

What would your perfect trip or vacation be like? Where would you go and for how long? Would you go to summer camp? Would you drive across the planet in a fancy supercar?

Look at Old Family Photos

Oh, man. Did you see what Mom's wearing? Wow. They wore funny clothes back when your parents were teens.

Solve a Mystery

Hmmm... where can we find a mystery? Oh, look! Someone left the crackers out on the counter again. Follow the trail of crumbs and try to figure out who left it there. And this odd sock... how did it end up under the couch cushions? Can you find any clues?

Mute the TV

Pretend you are the people on television. What is going on? What are they saying? Is it serious or silly? With the sound off, take over and say what you think they are saying (or aren't saying).

Dress Your Pet

Safety First: If your pet begins growling, hissing, or acting as though he or she is going to bite or scratch when you are trying to dress them up, give up. Trust me.

Shred a Newspaper

Feeling upset about something? Or just plain old silly? Take a newspaper and shred it! With your hands! With scissors! Let it all out!

Create a Puppet Show

If you don't have puppets you can make your own as well as a puppet theatre—instructions for both are found in the Construction Crafts section.

Make a Commercial

Do you have a favorite something you'd like to create a commercial for? Go for it! What do you love about it? What would other people like about it? Why should they buy it?

Act Out a Story

You can act out a story you've written, a book you like, or even your favorite TV show, or reenact a family adventure.

Record Yourself

Record yourself on a tape player making music, singing, talking, telling a story, or making funny sounds.

Webcam Visit

Cousins, grandparents, friends… who do you want to chat with? As well, places like ski hills or national monuments have webcams. Check one out—but be careful. Sometimes webcams are…inappropriate. This is an activity you want to do with an adult at the keyboard.

Safety First: Check out my online safety tips before surfing the net.

Have to Buy Something

Flip through a catalogue. Pretend you have to buy one thing from each page. What would you pick? What about your friends? Can you guess what they would pick?

Teddy Bear Bed

Using a cardboard box make a bed for your dolls or teddy bears.

Rice Sandbox

Toddler fun alert! A rice sandbox is an easy mini indoor sandbox. Simply place about a half inch of white rice in a cake pan and add some toy cars or trucks, a spoon, or other fun toys and let them play.

Is the rice getting boring? Add glass beads, a few unpopped popcorn kernels, or small stones for a new sensory experience.

Safety First: Don't add items that can be a choke hazard for your little ones. Glass beads and small stones are best suited for older children who have outgrown the habit of putting things in their mouths.

Space Aliens/Robots

Using a cardboard box, make a space helmet or robot mask. Have an adult cut a square out of the front of the box—this will be where you look through. This box will be your helmet or mask.

Paint the cardboard box any color you like and glue things such as buttons, pipe cleaners, yarn, shiny paper onto it to make it look like an alien or robot head.

Welcome to planet Earth.

Weatherman

Look outside and try to guess what today's weather will be. Write it down as well as what the weatherman predicted. At the end of the day, check back. Who was right? Wrong? Were you both close? Maybe you could be a weatherman when you grow up!

Mix Up Your Room

Safety First: Make sure a parent is around to help you with this one. Especially if you're moving big things or furniture—you don't want to get squished! No Flat Stanley's in this book!

Now… let's see… how about the bed over there and the dresser over here. And maybe move the books onto this shelf and the toys onto that one…

There. Much better. What do you think?

People Watching

This one is good for passing time when waiting for your parents. People watching can be done anywhere there are people (it might be out your front window, your school, just down the street or at the mall).

Watch the people go by. What are they wearing? How do they walk? What's their expression? Do they look lonely all by themselves?

Now let's get silly! Make up stories. What do these people do for a living? Are they nice or mean? How did the couples meet? (It's okay to be silly—Hey! Look at that couple that met at the circus, live at the North Pole, eat only broccoli, and used to work as elves for Santa!)

Have a Bath

Make it a bubble bath to up the fun factor! Wow. Was that a mermaid? Watch out for the submarine! Whoa! That wave came out of nowhere—sorry about the floor, Mom!

Reorganize

Can't find your stuff? Maybe you want things put in a different place? Reorganize! Take control! Reorganize anything! Your socks. Your books. Your games. Your music. Your toys. Your everything!

Roll Coins

Hint: You can get paper coin rolls at your bank for free.

Look at a Map

Look for interesting places you haven't heard of. Or look for places you've heard of, but don't know where they are.

Ghost Hunting

Can you find a ghost? Where do you think they live? What do they look like? Are they cold? Warm? Can they speak to you? Are they mischievous? Maybe they're the ones to blame for missing socks. By the way, do you think they would make a good invisible (or not so invisible) friend?

Tubular

Tape cardboard tubes together (mailing tubes, paper towel tubes, and/or wrapping paper tubes) and make long race tracks for marbles or small balls to run through!

Spy Code
To create a secret (spy) code, you will need a cipher.

Um… A what?

A thingy that will help you decode (unmix) your messages that are written in secret code—as well as write them. In other words, a decoder.

This is a simple code that rearranges the alphabet:
A=N B=O C=P D=Q E=R F=S G=T
H=U I=V J=W K=X L=Y M=Z
To use this code, the letter A becomes the letter N, and the letter N becomes A.

Try decoding this: Lbh qrpbqrq vg!

I Declare Myself _____ Give yourself a nickname.
You can make a nickname based on your real name. For example, Elizabeth sometimes becomes "Liz" or "Beth" or "Lizzy." What nicknames can you make from your name?

If you have a name that doesn't make many good nicknames (thanks, Mom & Dad!), try a nickname based on something you do well (or don't do well) or even something you like. Someone who smiles a lot might get nicknamed "Sunshine" or "Smiley." Or someone who *loooooves* pickles, might get nicknamed "The Pickleman." (It's happened. Trust me. Be careful what you wish for with nicknames!)

How about your friends and family—can you think of nicknames for them, too?

Meditate
Meditating is a form of relaxation. You can sit or lay quietly to meditate. Clear your mind the best you can. Focus on how your arms, legs, and body feel. Try to make your breath nice and relaxed. If you want, you can hum "mmmmmm" as you meditate.

Movie Night
Rent a movie or watch one of your own. Pretend you are at a movie theatre! Make popcorn, dim the lights, and invite some friends. (Check out the outside TV idea in the Outdoor Play section.)

Hint: If you are tired of your own movies, ask your parents if you can trade with a friend.

Reminisce

This means to think about the past. Remember that water fight last summer? Or when you learned to ride a bike? Or how about that time you cut your foot? You can start by thinking "I remember when…" Reminiscing with family and friends can be fun—adults like to reminisce a lot! (Check out the Word Games section for some goofy reminiscing games.)

Solitaire

There are tons of different versions of the card game, solitaire. Get someone to teach you the versions they know or look up more versions online or in a card game rule book from your local library.

Take a Nap

There. I said it. Close your eyes and drift away into daydreams, wishes, and eventually slumber.

More!

- Yoga
- Enter a Coloring Contest
- Jigsaw Puzzle
- Daydream
- Cuddle a Pet
- Play with a Pet
- Watch Fish Swim

Hug & Snuggle Someone

We all need a little physical affection sometimes and kids—especially boys—often don't get the physical reassurance they need from those around them. Hugs feel good and release chemicals in our bodies that not only bring us closer, but make us feel good. Having a tough day? Snag a hug from someone you love.

Even more…

- Phone Someone
- Take Photos
- Enter a Contest
- Make a Dragon Cave
- Draw a Map of Your House
- Ask a Relative to Tell You a Story About When They Were a Kid

How bored are you? The REAL test...

- Do Your Homework
- Do Your Chores
- Clean Your Room (Want to make it a game? Pick up all the big things first. Or, pick up a bunch of things in one color such as black, then move on to another color such as red, then on to another color until you're done.)

FASHION FUN

Since play comes in so many types, it teaches a wide array of skills and essentially trains children for just about anything life might throw their way.

Gabrielle Principe
Your Brain on Childhood

Clothing and accessories are a form of self-expression. Dress up, break a few clothing rules and have some fun!

Dress in Your Favorite Color
Can you wear all your favorite color—and no others—from your underwear to your hat?

Decorate Your Shoes
This works well with plain canvas shoes as you can paint on them with fabric paint or markers.

Decorate Your Shirt
Do you have a plain white shirt? Let's make it interesting! You can use all sorts of things to decorate a shirt—everything from iron-on photos you've printed off using your home computer and printer (you can find printable iron-ons in stationary stores), draw with fabric pens or paint, and more. Get creative! Also, check out the tie dye directions in the Artistic Play section.

Can you do this...
- Find a New Way to Lace Up Your Shoes
- Wear All of Your Clothes at Once
- Put Your Clothes on Inside Out
- Put Your Clothes on Backwards
- Make an Outfit Using a Towel and Safety Pins
- Make a Costume
- Do Your Best Runway Walk
- Buy Something Strange at a Second Hand Store and Wear it All Day
- Make Your Own Clothes
- Pajama Day
- Retro Outfit
- Dress Up as Someone Else

PLAYCATION DAY TRIP IDEAS

According to Stuart Brown, author of *Play: How it Shapes the Brain, Opens the Imagination, and Invigorates the Soul*, highly successful people have a rich play life. Hmm. I like the sound of that, don't you?

Brown says that free play—unstructured, unscripted, and unscheduled play—is good for adults, too. It helps us handle stress, combat depression, and prevents cognitive, emotional, and social narrowing. In other words, engaging in play expands who we are in a positive way—play isn't just for kids!

On a different note, quality family time is becoming increasingly rare as families become busier. If you're looking for ways to reconnect with your family, get off the couch, and out of the house, then look no further. This chapter is all about playcations—day trips around your local area that will be playfully fun for the *whole* family.

Grab the family and get ready to create some new family memories, prevent cognitive, emotional, and social narrowing (yikes!), and engage in some wonderful, playful bonding experiences! Let's go!

Go to...
- A Farmer's Market
- An Aquarium
- A Trade Show
- A Rodeo or Stampede
- A Concert
- A Video Arcade (Can you find one? They're getting harder and harder to find!)
- Watch a Play or Other Dramatic Performance
- A Theme Park/Amusement Park (*Hint:* Search online for coupons!)
- A Festival
- Watch a Parade
- Planetarium
- Science Center

Visit a Museum
What are you into? Art? Dinosaurs? Old Farm Machinery? There might be a museum dedicated to all the things you love!

Watch a Movie in a Movie Theatre
Matinees (afternoon shows) and Tuesdays often offer discount admittance and some movie theatres even offer kids afternoons where they only dim the theatre lights instead of turning them off so kids don't get scared.

Visit a Senior Citizens Home
Know someone in an old folks home? They often don't get many visitors and would love to see you! Call first to make sure it's a good time.

Visit a Children's Museum

Children's museums are built with kids in mind! They have tons of interactive displays that kids are encouraged to touch, climb on, and play with unlike regular museums. So if you have extra bouncy, curious kids who like to touch, touch, touch, take them to a children's museum and set their curiosity loose!

Take a Bus Somewhere New

Is there somewhere in your city or local area that you've always wanted to check out? Satisfy that curiosity! Grab the bus and check it out.

Safety First: Bring an adult with you.

Go to the Zoo

If the zoo is far away, take a look around locally. There may be a private petting zoo that allows guests. They may charge a fee, but it will likely be less than a big city zoo, plus you might get to pet some of the animals!

Get active...
- Mini-golf
- Golf
- Indoor Climbing Wall
- Rock Climbing
- Zipline
- Hiking
- Go for a Nature Walk Along an Interpretive Trail at a Nature Center
- Horseback Riding/Pony Rides
- Get Lost in a Corn Maze or Other Type of Outdoor Maze
- Laser Tag
- Paintball
- Bowling
- White Water Rafting

Go to a Dollar Store

See what treasures you can find for a dollar or two.

Go to an Auction

Guess who buys what and how much they will pay.

Go to a Kids Camp

There are all sorts of camps for kids. There are day camps that last only a few hours during the day to sleep away camps that can last all summer. Many cities and towns now have camps or organized activities for kids when there is no school—during holidays or professional development days.

Go to a Family Camp

Take the whole family!

Go to a Garage Sale/Yard Sale

For a challenge take $5 or $10 and see who can get the coolest thing. Or, look for something specific—like a scavenger hunt. For example, try to find a funny looking hat for less than $2 or find something exactly like what you have at home.

Make a Wish

Throw pennies in a wishing well or fountain and make a wish! Make sure there aren't any fish in the fountain or wishing pond as coins can make them sick.

Play Tourist in Your Hometown

If you were a tourist, where would you go? What would you take pictures of?

Check out the Library

Take a look around. Libraries often have events for youngsters that are free or close to it. As well, they have magazines, computers, music, audiobooks, movies, and lots of great books! If you can't find what you want or need ask a librarian to help you out.

Go for a Drive

Back in the 1950s, when cars were still sort of a neat-o idea, people would go for a Sunday drive where they would leisurely explore their local area, visiting places they had never seen before. What area are you curious about and would like to see? Are they building a new subdivision? Did the river flood somewhere near you recently? A lake dry up? Go check it out with your family.

Safety First: You'll need an adult to do the driving, of course!

Visit an Art Gallery

Which painting or sculpture is your favorite? What do you think the artist was thinking when he or she created that piece of art?

Window Shopping

Window shopping is when you look in the windows of stores—but you don't go in and you don't buy anything. Just look at the interesting things that are on display in the windows.

Pick a Place on a Map and Go There

Safety First: Take an adult with you! (And maybe bring a picnic, too!)

Watch Construction

Are they building something near you? Machines digging a hole? Paving a road? Building a skyscraper or new house?

Safety First: Make sure you stay behind the construction area fence and stay out of the way of machines—constructions sites can be dangerous and they are not for playing in EVER.

Watch a Sport Being Played

Outdoor, live sports are the best!

Watch Some Motorized Fun...

- Motocross Event
- Stock Car Racing
- Crash Up Derby
- Monster Truck Rally
- Go-Cart Track (Join the fun!)
- Tractor Pull
- ATV or Quad Ride (*Safety First:* Always wear a helmet and have an adult drive)

Visit Animals in a Pet Store or Animal Shelter

Take Something to the Dump or Recycling Center

Where does all of our stuff go after we are done with it? Can you recycle the item? Give it away? Throw it away? Where does it go when you are done with it? Go check it out!

Check it Out

Check your local newspaper or community online to see what community activities are going on or coming up. Festival? Fair? Market? Events for kids? Parades?

Horse Races
Which horse will win the race? Which jockey's colors do you like best?

Hint: Ask if you can visit the barns to see the horses and riders. Sometimes you can at special times.

Geocaching
Geocaching is a sport that uses a GPS (Global Positioning Satellite) receiver to find a hidden cache (a small container that contains a logbook and sometimes trinkets for trading). If you don't have a GPS (smart phones have them now) or know of one you can borrow, you may be able to rent one from a sporting goods rental place.

To find a hidden geocache near you, log onto www.geocaching.com. Search for nearby caches and download the cache's longitude and latitude coordinates into your GPS. (There is an app for smart phones.) The website has more information as well as rules. It is a great way to get outside and enjoy a nice treasure hunt!

WhereIGo
Similar to geocaching (above activity), but a bit more involved. Find out more on the WhereIGo website: www.whereigo.com.

Waymarking
Waymarking is like geocaching, but without the caches. Around the world people have marked spots using the earth's longitude and latitude coordinates (a GPS will help you find them). Marked spots might be a nice view, an interesting building or even a mural. Find out more at www.waymarking.com.

Story Time
Local library or bookstores often have free (or very low cost) story time for kids. Phone ahead to see when story time is held and if there is a cost/registration required to attend.

Go for Ice-Cream or Some Other Treat

OUTSIDE PLAY

The brain is better able to pay attention, hold things in memory, and show self-control after it has been outdoors.

Gabrielle Principe
Your Brain on Childhood

According to some researchers, our most recent generation of children might be the first American generation since World War II that will die at an earlier age than their parents (due to lifestyle factors). Let's allow that to sink in. Our children might have a *shorter* life expectancy than *we* do. That's shocking and turns my gut. Yours, too?

The good news is that it's *easy* to fix. The problem? Overall, we have become a sedentary society. We eat quickly, and we eat food that has been heavily processed. Our bodies were not designed for this and probably never will be. And it's affecting our children. But we can turn it around. Try committing to fewer activities that have your family running like crazy (I know, I know. It's *hard*. But keep reading—you're already on the right track). Also eat as a family (a lack of family meals is a significant indicator when it comes to identifying unhealthy marriages and unhealthy, unhappy teens). As well, cook food that doesn't require ripping open a bag (unless the bag contains flash-frozen veggies with no additives). Finally, get active. (I'm not saying join a gym—although that's good, too—but restrict screen time and introduce more physical activity such as family walks, bike rides, or whatever makes your family grin (see the previous chapter for "playcation" day trip ideas). If all else fails, get a dog who demands walks—it worked for us.

What else? According to Richard Louv, author of the eye-opening book *Last Child in the Woods*, says that children are more physically active when outside (note that he doesn't say in organized sports). As well, children who play among trees, rocks, and an uneven ground have better monitor fitness especially in terms of balance and agility. On top of the physical benefits, time in nature leads to stress reduction, better mental health (such as feeling less anxious, angry, and/or depressed), as well as diminishes the rate of physical or emotional illness, minimizes ADHD symptoms, and leads to better concentration as well as mental acuity. When children play outdoors they are often given more independence which, in turn, increases feelings of self-worth and confidence. This then boosts their social skills as well as resiliency against stress and adversity.

A natural nature bonus: It's also naturally sensory. In fact, alienation from nature leads to a diminished use of the senses. As humans we need to taste, see, hear, and touch to reconnect with our senses so if you're worried about sensory play, nature is your play place.

P.S. Curious if there are benefits to allowing your children to play outside unsupervised—within reason, of course. Check out the infographic at the back of this book.

Build a Tree House
You're going to need adult help with this one. There are great plans at hardware stores plus any supplies you need. Check out the library or online for building plans.

Build an Outdoor Fort
Outdoor forts are the best and can be anything from a secret spy hideout to a fairy nest to a dragon cave or a clubhouse. Good fort spots might be a hideout under or between big bushes, a hollow spot in the hedge, under the deck, or... anywhere!

Make a Fairy House
Make a tiny house for a fairy and see if one comes to live there. They are shy, so you'll have to be really, really quiet.

Fairies like their homes to be built in wooded areas and out of natural materials. That means no plastics, rubber, or metals. They like leaves, nuts, berries, flowers, shells, pine cones, and other naturally beautiful building materials. They also like their homes to be made from leaves that have fallen off trees by themselves. They don't like it when their builders use flowers that are still growing, trees that are stripped off live trees and that sort of thing.

Watch the Sunrise/Sunset
Does the world seem different at this time of day? What colors do you see in the sky?

Look for Fossils
Don't have fossils in your area? Mix up some mud, pop some plastic dinosaur figurines in it, and let the mud dry. Once the mud has set, go on an excavation! Can you find any dinosaurs? (This one will appeal to toddlers up to older kids. And maybe adults, too!)

Hint: Don't have the patience to let the mud dry? Hide your dinosaurs in the sandbox or a cake tray filled with rice (find the rice sandbox play idea in the Kids Stuff section). Then excavate your fossils! You can use basting brushes, spoons, and other kitchen tools if you want to get 'official' like a real paleontologist (dinosaur expert) and have some tools.

Find Cloud Animals
Lie on your back and look at the clouds—whoa! Is that a giraffe?

Watch TV Outside
Take your TV outside and watch! (Make sure you ask first.) Everything too "tied up?" How about a portable DVD player? Maybe use a projector to project against the garage door?

Family movie night is moving outside this week! Invite the whole neighborhood!

Build a Rocket

Kits are available for building toy rockets or you can go big and build your own from scratch.

Safety First: Make sure you have an adult help build and launch your rocket. Ready to launch? Make sure you are in an open area where there isn't more than a very light breeze and there are no trees. (We still have a rocket stuck in a treetop! Learn from our mistakes.)

Start a Rock Collection

What kind of rocks can you find in your yard? At the park? Want to know what kind of rocks they are? There are rock identification guides online, in apps, as well as handy books.

Wash the Car

Do you have a bucket, hose, and sponge? Wash the car as a surprise for your parents. You could also go with your family to a drive-thru car wash, or a place where you wash it with a wand.

Jump on a Trampoline

Safety first: Be careful! Trampolines are one of the biggest sources of childhood injuries. While safety nets help, accidents still happen. Be careful of others on the trampoline and if it feels dangerous… it is. Don't. Do. It.

Stilts

Don't have stilts? Make some out of hockey sticks or wood. Look for instructions at the library or on the Internet. They are a TON of fun!

Draw on the Sidewalk with Chalk

Don't have sidewalk chalk? There is a recipe in the Mad Scientist's section.

Try and Catch Your Shadow

Can you catch it?

Look for Egg Shells

Is it spring? Baby birds hatching? You might find their old shells on the ground under trees where they have nests. We used to always find pale blue eggs from robins and speckled egg shells from sparrows.

Water Balloon Fight

Fill a balloon with water, by holding the end over the tap. Tie it off and give it a toss (outside of course).

Hint: There are special balloons made especially for water balloon fights, but you can use regular balloons, too. Or rubber gloves… or sandwich bags… or…

Catch Butterflies

You must be gentle with butterflies and moths. They have a layer of special dust that coats their wings that is needed for their health and ability to fly.

Catch Bugs

After you are done watching them, make sure you let them go. Also make sure you have small air holes in your bug containers so your bugs have enough oxygen.

Animals…

- Take a Dog for a Walk
- Play Fetch with a Dog
- Look for the First Robin of Spring

Track an Animal

When animals walk through fresh snow, mud, soft sand, or dirt they leave foot tracks. In most areas, bird, dog, cat, and people tracks are fairly easy to find. Maybe you will even find raccoon, deer, or bear tracks. Where did the animal go? Follow them to find out—just keep your eyes open as you might bump into the animal itself if the tracks are fresh enough.

Wonder what kind of animal tracks you see? Look them up online or in an animal tracks book.

Safety first: Watch out! Wild animals can be dangerous—give them lots of room and stay far away from them. Never feed or approach a wild animal even if it looks friendly.

Bird Watching

Curious about a bird you saw? Look it up in a bird guide. I have a great app right now that is excellent for identifying the birds in my area.

Make a Stick Hut/Shelter
Can you make a house out of branches and sticks?

Make a Lemonade Stand and Sell Lemonade
If it isn't good weather for selling lemonade, you can make the stand now and sell the lemonade some other time. You can also sell other things at your stand too, such as artwork or homemade crafts. All you need is lemonade, cups, a table, a sign, and a busy place to catch foot traffic. (Selling lemonade at your family's yard sale is a good way to find customers!)

Camping
If your family camps in an RV, ask if you can camp beside it in a tent. Bring a friend for extra fun. Not going anywhere soon? Try camping in your backyard.

Bonfire/Campfire
A bonfire is a large fire. You can make a small fire in a fire pit.

Safety First: Never play with or around a fire. Make sure an adult sets up and lights the fire. Also make sure you have water handy to put out the fire.

Tell Scary Stories Around Your Fire

Sing Campfire Songs Around the Fire
If you don't know any campfire songs, ask your parents or grandparents if they know some. I'll bet they do. If all else fails, everyone probably knows the national anthem.

Wiener Roast
How's that fire looking? Shall we cook some hot dogs on a roasting stick? (Check out the Spider Dogs instructions in the Food Fun section as well as how to toast marshmallows over a fire.)

Safety First: Fire safety is super important when near a fire. Make sure you have an adult help you with the fire as well as cooking.

Fly a Kite
Safety First: Make sure you fly kites away from power lines and trees. If your kite gets caught in something, make sure you let go of the string and go get an adult to help you get your kite down.

Lawn Bowling/Bocce Ball

You will need: You will need at least 5 balls (4 the same size and 1 that is smaller) and 2 players.

Bocce Ball and Lawn Bowling are slightly different, but the basic idea in both games is that you want to get as close to the "jack" with your own balls without touching it. The closest player wins.

The small ball will be the "jack" and at the start of the game it is placed in the grassy playing area. Players stand behind a line. (Decide how far away is easiest for your players and their ages. It might be four feet away from the "jack" or it might be as far as twenty feet away.) Players then toss or roll their balls across the grass, trying to get their ball as close to the "jack" as they can without bumping it. The closest player wins. If you hit the "jack" that ball doesn't count and is removed from the field.

Get active, get outdoors…
- Mountain Biking (Don't have mountains? Hit the hills!)
- Run
- Go for a Walk
- Bike Ride
- Kick a Small Stone Down the Sidewalk
- Ride a Scooter
- Pogo Stick
- In-line Skating/Rollerskating
- Skateboarding
- Archery
- Horseshoes
- Ring Toss (Make your own rings out of plastic container lids. Then shove a stick into the ground to toss them onto!)
- Hopscotch
- Play Catch
- Four Square
- Tetherball

RAIN PLAY

More awesome outdoor play—but this play needs rain. Check the forecast, put on your rubber boots and go splash!

Play & Explore!
- Count the Worms that Came Out in the Rain
- Jump in Mud Puddles
- Make Mud Pies
- Go for a Walk in the Rain
- Look for a Rainbow and a Pot of Gold

Count Thunder

You'll need a thunderstorm for this one! Look out your window and watch for lightning. When you see it flash across the sky, begin counting until you hear the accompanying thunder. (Thunder is the sound caused by lightning.) Count slowly, one-one thousand, two-one thousand, three-one thousand… until the thunder comes. Take the number you counted to and divide it by 5. That's how many miles away the lightning is from you. Some people don't divide by 5, and since we're just having fun, you don't have to either—unless you want to.

Safety First: During a thunderstorm, stay out from under trees, the water and other areas that attract lightning.

Toothpick Races

Race twigs or toothpicks in puddles or little puddle streams made by the rain. Which one is the fastest?

Make Rivers Between Puddles

Can you join two puddles together? Drag the heel of your rubber boot, or use a stick to dig a trench between two puddles and watch them join together.

Smell The Rain

Ahhhh. Doesn't it smell *amazing*?

Rain Paintings

Drop food coloring on a piece of cardboard or paper plate. Place it out in the rain. The rain will splash the food coloring, making it spread as well as mixing the colors. When the picture is as mixed as you want it to be, pull it inside and let it dry.

Tip: If it's raining hard, the rain will splash the food coloring—be careful, it stains clothes… and maybe your deck or front step, too.
Variation: No rain in the forecast? Use a spray bottle filled with water.

PLAYGROUND FUN

Play is how we are made, how we develop and adjust to change.

Stuart Brown
Play

A place with "play" right in its name. How awesome is that?

Psst! Want an interesting fact? According to Richard Louv (author of *Last Child in the Woods*) when children live in a place where they can play outside they typically have two times as many friends as children who don't play outside. So, if you want your kids to make friends, get them outside and a playground is an excellent place to start!

Go to the Playground

If there is a kid there that you do not know, introduce yourself! You may make a new friend.

Go to a New Playground or Park

Is there a playground you drive by but have never been to? Try it out. You might just find a new favorite. The kids and I gave ourselves a playground challenge a few summers ago where we tried to go to every playground in our hometown... after about thirteen different playgrounds we gave up the challenge, but we did find some new favorites!

Try Going Over-Bars on the Swings

Monster

A playground version of tag—only the "it" player is a monster! ROAR!

One player stays on the ground and is the "monster." Everyone else climbs the monkey bars and tries to stay out of the monster's reach. The players on the monkey bars must keep moving. Once the monster touches one of the players, they become the new monster. If a player drops onto the ground, they are the new monster.

Charlie Brown

This is played on a teeter totter (if you find one!). One player is Charlie Brown and picks a color. They keep the other player in the air until they are able to guess the color. It goes like this:

While in the air, the non-Charlie Brown player says: "Charlie Brown, Charlie Brown, please let me down." Charlie Brown replies: "Not until you guess my favorite color." The other player guesses until they get it right. Then, once the color has been guessed, they are let down and become Charlie Brown.

Give an Under Whale

An under whale is a big, whooshy underduck. What's an underduck? It's a giant push where you run and duck under the swing at the last moment.

What other animal pushes can you give? Hummingbird? (Quick and little.) Elephant? (Big and loud.) Snake? (Wiggly and hissy.) For added fun, make the animal noises while giving the push.

Grounders

Blind tag on the playground equipment—this is for older kids (although the younger kids cheat and peek to stay safe, which I am definitely okay with them doing as are the older kids if they're not too obvious about it).

One person is "it." While they are "it," they have to keep their eyes closed while they try to tag other players unless they are on the ground. Then they can open their eyes to see where everyone is on the playground equipment. But as soon as they are back up on the equipment, they have to close their eyes. Players can touch the ground, but only for three seconds—and if the "it" players notices, they yell, "Grounders!" and the person on the ground is now "it."

There are almost as many variations for this game as there are playgrounds.

Note: This game is nerve-wracking for parents, but kids love it and, surprisingly, don't take as many crazy risks as you'd think. Having their eyes closed actually forces them to be *more* careful than they would be regularly. (Studies show that children who play on irregular surfaces tend to have fewer accidents as they have to pay more attention.) But really? Kids secretly peek when they feel as though they might be in a risky spot. *Shh!* Don't tell them I saw them.

MOTHER EARTH OUTDOOR PLAY

Nature inspires creativity in a child by demanding visualization and the full use of the senses.

Richard Louv
Last Child in the Woods

Here's an interesting fact presented by Richard Louv in his book *Last Child in the Woods*, researchers believe that mental health improves and is preserved by digging in dirt. Well, now. That sounds a lot like childhood, doesn't it? Maybe we should join in!

Growing Tipi

You will need: three bamboo sticks (or regular wood stakes or sticks—about 3 feet long (1 meter)), climbing plants (like sweet peas, beans, hops, or ivy), dirt, twine, three cans or plant pots.

Place dirt and one stick in each pot. Angle the sticks so they aren't quite straight up—they are going to lean over and touch the other two pot sticks later. Place the pots in a circle (triangle, really) and tie the tops of the sticks together. Plant your seeds in the pots and as they start to grow, wind them up the sticks, forming a living tipi. You can build this one outside, inside, or even on the balcony of an apartment. Is the tipi big enough someone can hide in it? Maybe fairies, teddy bears, or dragons?

Rhubarb Leaf Hat

The leaves of rhubarb plants make excellent hats.

Safety First: Don't eat the leaf as it is poisonous.

Grow a Vegetable/Plant a Garden

Don't have a plot of land? Grow them in a pot on your balcony or near your window. Window gardening is an idea that is taking off everywhere! (We currently have lettuce growing in a pot on our front step. Easy. Convenient. Yummy.)

Grass Whistle

Place your hands in the prayer position (palm to palm). Hold a piece of grass (a wide piece is best) tightly between your thumbs. Now blow through the tiny space created between your thumbs and the grass. The grass should vibrate and make a whistling sort of noise. It might take some practice and experimenting with different grass pieces as well as how you hold the grass. Don't give up!

Wax a Leaf

You will need: leaves, wax paper, newspaper, iron, and adult to help.

Place a leaf between two pieces of wax paper. Then, place the wax paper between two pieces of plain paper or newspaper so the wax doesn't come off on your iron in the next step.

Safety First: Have an adult iron the stack of papers. The wax from the wax paper should melt over the leaf, preserving it and its color.

Dry Flowers
To dry flowers, hang them upside down by a piece of string tied around the stem. Sometimes spraying them with hairspray helps preserve them.

Press Flowers
Place flowers between two pieces of newspaper. Put a flat, heavy object like a big book on top of the paper until the flowers are dry (a day or two). The book will press the flowers flat as they dry.

Once dry, glue the flowers onto a homemade card, a memory box (instructions found in the Artistic Play section) or simply admire how amazingly flat they are.

Collect Leaves or Pine Cones
Can you make some cool nature crafts and pictures with them? Make an animal by gluing leaves to a piece of paper in the shape of the animal. Make a tree with your leaves. Glue googly eyes on the pine cones to make owls… What else can you do with them?

Web Work
Watch a spider spin its web. Does it make a circle web or a different kind of web? (Did you know some spiders will make webs larger than a city bus? Wow! That's a lot of work… and a lot of bug lunch!) Where does your spider start first? Does it take in some of its web as it works?

Blow the Fuzzy Seeds off Dandelions

Pop the Heads off Dandelions

Daisy Chain & Daisy Crown
You will need about 10-12 daisies with their stems attached. With each daisy, make a small slit in the stem a little way down from the blossom (about an inch (2.5 cm)). You can use your fingernail or a plastic knife.

Thread one daisy stem through the hole you made in another stem. You will now have two daisies threaded together. Add a third daisy by feeding its stem through the second flower in the chain.

Keep adding daisies until your chain is the length you need. Then tuck the ends together in a circle and you'll have a crown, necklace, or bracelet/anklet.

Dandelion Stem Necklace

Collect a handful of dandelions, trying to pick as much stem as you can. Take the blossoms off your stems so you have a pile of stems.

Push the smaller end of one stem into the larger end to form a circle with the stem. You now have one loop. Feed the next stem through that loop before closing it like you did with the first stem. You should now have two interlocked stem loops. Keep going until you have enough interconnected loops to make a necklace, then link the last stem loop through the first loop on the chain and the last loop on the chain to form one big necklace.

Sunflower Hut

Grow sunflowers close together in your garden to make a little hut for kids under the big leaves.

More fun!

- Jump in a Pile of Leaves
- Climb a Tree
- Look for the First Flower of Spring or the Last Flower of Fall
- Look for a Four-Leaf Clover
- Pick Fruit (Don't have any? Look for a U-Pick farm where you can pick your own fruit!)
- Make a Nest out of Sticks or Grass
- Decorate a Tree (What can you decorate it with?)
- Make a Wreath
- Stop and Smell Flowers
- Pick Flowers

Nature Picture

What do you have handy to make nature art?

Rocks or shells could be arranged on the seashore's sand to make a picture of a mermaid. Stones, sticks, or pine cones could be used to create a picture frame in the dirt, then use a stick as your pencil to draw a picture inside your frame. Or create your nature picture by laying leaves and sticks in ways that make animal shapes. (Leaves could be bodies and sticks could be used as legs and tails.) What else can you use?

Nature's Paintbrushes & Water Paintings

Make your own paintbrush out of leaves or grass. Paint with water on the sidewalk or rocks. How many different brushes can you discover today? How are they different?

Start a Plant from a Seed or Cutting

Sometimes you can start a new houseplant by cutting a piece off a big one. For most plants, stick the cutting in water until it grows roots. There are some that can be stuck straight in the dirt after being cut and they will grow! What can you grow?

Terrarium

A terrarium is a small, closed container for plants—essentially, you're creating your own mini atmosphere for the plants.

You will need: a jar (the wider the better) or a fishbowl, lid or clear plastic wrap, potting soil, plants, water.

Place about 2 inches (5 cm) of soil in the bottom of your container. Plant seeds or place plant cuttings in the soil. Generally with a terrarium, you can cut a piece of plant stem that has leaves and place the stem straight into the terrarium's soil and it will grow, even if it doesn't have roots. But not always—experiment or research your type of plant to find out if it will work.

Once planted, lightly water your plants or seeds until the soil is damp—but not really wet. Place a lid on your terrarium or cover the opening with cling wrap or a small plate.

In time, the plants will grow. Because they are in a sealed container, they will need to be watered only once or twice a year. If it gets really wet and mildewy in the jar, you may have to remove the lid for a day or two to let it dry out a little bit.

Fun Tidbit: Add plastic shark toys or fish, seashells, or other items such as toy dinosaurs in your terrarium.

Rock Stacker

How many rocks, pebbles, or stones can you stack on top of each other before they fall over? Are some better than others for stacking?

Inuksuk

Inuksuit originated in the Canadian Arctic. These rock statues look like people and are used to help hunters find their way like street signs.

Good inuksuk rocks are flat—both on top and bottom. Stack rocks on top of each other to build a person—an inuksuk. You can make an Inuksuk as big or as small as you like. If you are making a tiny inuksuk, you can glue the rocks together and bring it inside.

Rock Pens

Sandstone is a soft stone and can be used to write on itself. Can you find rocks that will write on each other?

Charcoal Pens

Safety First: Have an adult help you place the end of a small stick in the hot coals of a fire for a minute or two. Pull it out and let it cool. Careful, it's hot!

You now have a charcoal pen! Can you draw on rocks and other surfaces?

Tip: Charcoal can stain, so be careful where you write with your new pen.

Draw on Birch Bark

You have to be careful when you pull bark off trees so you don't kill or injure the tree. It is best to pull bark off a dead tree or the thin bark that is already being naturally shed.

Draw on a Fungus

Fungi that grow on trees are great to draw on when they are fresh (the part that faces down is white and soft making it easy to draw on). When it dries out, it hardens, making your drawing permanent.

Make a Worm Hotel

Q: What did the worm mom say to her son when he was late for supper?
A: Where IN earth have you been?

What do worms like? Dirt! Make 'em a hotel and see if you can find some worms to add to it.

Nature's Boats
Make a homemade boat out of things you find along the shore. Reeds, driftwood, even long grass can make a great boat. Got your boat ready? Check out the next activity!

Safety First: Never play around the water without adult supervision.

Race your Boats
Did you make a boat out of shoreline discoveries such as in the above activity? Well, let's race them!

Or maybe you already have a boat you've made from something else or have a toy boat you want to race… Either way, bring your boats to the local puddle, pond, or lake. Don't want to lose your boat if it floats away? Tie a string or fishing line to it so you can pull it back if it drifts too far.

Safety First: Never play around the water without adult supervision.

SAND PLAY

One of the powers of play is that it gets us to exercise our bodies as well as our minds.

David Elkind
The Power of Play

You can do these activities at the beach or in the sandbox. Playing with different textures promotes tactile awareness and is naturally sensory as well as creative.

Bury Your Legs in the Sand
Ah! You have no legs! Oh, there they are. Whew! I was worried for a moment.

Bury a Friend in the Sand
Safety First: Don't cover their face. Also, don't pile too much on them as sand is heavy and can make it hard for them to breathe.

Find the Water Line
Near the shore of a lake or ocean, dig a hole—maybe only a foot away from the water's edge. How deep do you have to dig before the bottom of the hole fills with water?

Wow! How did that water get in there? You just found the water line where water is hanging out just waiting to be found.

Dig a Big Hole
At the beach, in the garden, in the snow, in the leaves, in the mud, in the sandbox, in your mashed potatoes... the possibilities are almost endless.

Safety First: Be careful! Big holes can cave in on themselves and sand is heavy and dangerous when there is lots of it.

Sandcastles
You will need damp sand. If the sand is too dry, add water until it packs into shapes without crumbling.

Pack sand into containers (yogurt containers, ice-cream pails and margarine containers work well), then dump them upside down to make different sandcastle shapes.

Sand Creature/Sculpture
Using your hands, pack damp sand into whatever shape you'd like. Using a small shovel, stick, or your hands, carve and shape details into your sculpture. Turtles are easy to shape and you can decorate its shell with seashells or simply use your finger to carve in shell details into its sand shell.

Sand Angel
Like snow angels, but you make them in the sand. Lie on your back and sweep your arms and legs up and down in the sand. Stand up and see your sand angel.

Write Messages in the Sand

It is best to have wet, packed sand like on the shore of a lake or ocean. Take a stick or your finger and write away! How much can you write before the waves come and wash it away?

Make Sand Roads and Sand Cities

Sand Chair

Carve and pack damp sand into a chair shape. Can you make one big enough for yourself or does it break when you try to sit on it?

WATER PLAY

> As children engage in water play, they are learning the many different ways that water can be the same but different... Water is endlessly fascinating to young children because it serves many different functions.
>
> David Elkind
> The Power of Play

I know sometimes playing in water is messy, and more work for the parent, but kids absolutely adore playing with one of our planet's most mysterious elements. This section is one big play-induced experiment. Let's get wet, let's get dirty, let's play and discover the world.

Safety First:
*** **ALWAYS follow your family's water safety rules when you play around water.** ***

Water Fight
Use the garden hose, wet sponges, a squeeze bottle, balloons, water guns, whatever you can find!

Skip Stones
There are three tricks to skipping stones along the water's surface.

1) Find a stone that fits nicely in your hand and isn't too big or heavy. A good skipping stone is flat on the bottom and slightly rounded on top.

2) You need a quiet lake, pond, or river that doesn't have lots of waves. The calmer and flatter the water surface, the better chance you have of your stone skipping along the water's surface.
Safety First: Watch out for people and animals.

3) It's all about your technique. You don't have to be tall or strong or a superhero, you just have to be patient until you have the knack. Here's how to develop that special stone tossing knack: Stand sideways to the water with your throwing arm away from the water. You're going to throw sidearm—across your body with your arm moving across your belly region as you wind up and toss. Your arm is going to stay at waist level the whole time. It might feel weird at first. (We throw sidearm for stone skipping so the rock is already going the direction you want it to go—bouncing across the water surface and not down and into the water.)

Give your knees a slight bend and draw your throwing arm back with the stone between your thumb and pointer finger (also known as your nose-picking finger). Make sure the flat side of your stone is facing down. Now whip that rock out there!

Did it skip? Probably not the first time. Keep practicing until your arm falls off—that's about the time you'll get this just perfect and get one to skip, skip… plop.

Got it down? See how many times you can get your stone to skip. If you're on a narrow, quiet river or creek see if you can get your stone to skip all the way to the shore on the other side.

Search for Sea Glass

Sea glass is a piece of broken glass that has been worn down by sand and waves in the ocean. Instead of having sharp edges, they're now smooth and rounded. Sometimes you can find bits of pottery washed up on the shore too.

Collect Seashells

Dig for Clams

Body Surfing

To body surf, you need some good waves along the shore. The ocean or a wave pool works well for this.

You will need to stand where the waves start to break near the shore (the waves start to roll down on themselves making the top of the wave turn white). You don't need super big waves, just big enough to push you back to shore if you ride them right.

Face the beach and wait for a wave to start breaking. Get in front of the breaking wave and start swimming. If you time it right, the wave will push you onto the beach. Watch out for sand in your bathing suit!

Safety First: Make sure an adult is watching in case you run into trouble. You also must be able to swim well—and a life jacket is also a good idea, even for good swimmers as the extra flotation will make it easier to ride the waves.

Bombs Away

While standing on shore, try to hit floating sticks or driftwood with stones from the shore. Who can hit the stick first? Bombs away! Splash!

River Stick Races

Each person drops a stick in the river at the same time to start the race. See which stick goes the fastest. If you have a bridge you can stand on, drop your stick off one side and see whose stick comes out the other side first. (This can work in small ponds, too.)

Safety First: Be careful as rivers can be fast and dangerous with slippery shores that can pitch you into the current faster than you can say, "Uh-oh!" Remember to always follow your family's water safety rules.

Float Down a River

Safety First: Wear a lifejacket even if you're in an inner tube. Also make sure an adult comes with you and check the river for hazards (like waterfalls and dams!) before you go.

Look for Tadpoles

In the spring check out your local pond, quiet stream or creek to see if you can find tadpoles.

Go…
- Windsurfing
- Waterskiing/Knee Boarding/Wakeboarding
- Rafting
- Surfing
- Jet skiing
- For a Boat Ride
- Sailing
- Paddle Boating
- Paddle Boarding
- Boogie Boarding
- Waterslides or Spray Park
- Swimming
- Canoeing
- Kayaking
- Fishing
- Snorkeling
- To the Beach

Slip and Slide

Use a ready-made slip and slide or create your own out of a long sheet of plastic and a garden hose.

Put on your bathing suit, pick out a smooth piece of lawn, put down the plastic, grab the hose or a bucket of water to wet the plastic and start sliding.

Hint: You may have to peg the plastic down at the starting point so it doesn't slide with you.

Water Polo
Water polo is kind of like soccer, but in the water. Players try to get the ball (they can use their hands) into nets at the other end of the swimming pool.

Marco Polo
This game is played in the swimming pool. One person is "it" and they try to catch other players. The tricky part is that the "it" player has to keep their eyes closed the whole time they are "it." (The other players can keep their eyes open.)

The person who is "it," yells "Marco," and the rest of the players reply, "Polo." Once "it" tags another player, they become "it." If someone doesn't reply "Polo" and "it" notices, that player then becomes "it" (unless they were under water when they were supposed to reply).

Variations: People who are not "it" can get out of the pool, but still have to keep one part of their body in the pool. If the "it" person thinks someone is out of the pool, they can yell "fish out of water" and whomever is out of the pool becomes "it."

OR if it is too challenging for the "it" players to remain blind the whole time, they can open their eyes when they touch the side of the pool. As soon as they let go, they have to close their eyes again.

More!
- Run Through the Sprinkler
- Underwater Somersault
- Underwater Handstand
- Pretend You Are a Dolphin/Shark/Whale
- Pretend You Are a Mermaid

Chase Waves Along the Shore
Did they get you? Better be fast!

Car Wash for Toys
Indoors or out, hand your child the garden hose, or set them up at the kitchen sink with a dish brush and their toys. This is a great game to play after the Tire Tracks Painting game found in the Paint Play section.

Hand Water Gun
Make a fist with your hand so your thumb is at the top of your fist just like you're going to have a thumb war with someone. Put your hand under the water (bath tubs or swimming pools are great) so the top part of your hand just pops above the surface. Now open your fist slightly (under water) and quickly squeeze your hand closed again while pressing your thumb down against your fist. Water that came into your fist should now come squirting out. Oops! Did you get yourself?

Bring the Water Indoors
Bring it inside! This is an easy, fun boredom buster for toddlers and preschoolers.

Fill a shallow bucket, cake pan, or sink with water and let the kids splash around with toy boats and other items in the water.

Hint: Place a towel under the bucket or pan. And if your child is playing in the sink, place a folded towel on the counter between your child and the basin to help catch those inevitable splashes and tidal waves.

Water Shoot Out
This boredom buster is a fun birthday party game you'll want to play every day.

Place several water-filled bottles (with no lids) on an outdoor table. Rest one ping pong ball on each bottle mouth and try to shoot them off using a squirt gun or the garden hose. Can you get them all?

DARK PLAY

Look inward for guidance and direction on what is best for your child and your family.

David Elkind
The Power of Play

Bending the rules and pushing through limits should happen within the realm of play. They aren't the dark side of play—they are the essence of play.

Stuart Brown
Play

Children often miss what nature has to offer after dark due to bedtimes and natural habits. These activities remind us what is offered after the sun goes down and that, sometimes, in order to have the society we want, we have to be the first ones to take the steps to make it happen. Take back the night, my friends.

———————————

Enjoy the Northern Lights/Southern Lights

Catch a Firefly

Star Gazing
Learn more about stars and planets at your local observatory (a place with a large, high-powered telescope—sometimes they have nights where the general public can come and look through their big telescopes), in an astronomy book or online. The best viewing is done away from big cities and towns where streetlights interfere with seeing the stars.

Hint: Check to see if there is a dark sky preserve near you—they don't allow lights so you can see the stars!
Double Hint: Don't have a telescope? Sometimes you can see some pretty amazing things with binoculars!

Admire the Moon
Is it full? Waxing? (Getting bigger?) Waning? (Getting smaller?) Get out your binoculars or a telescope. Can you see the moon's craters? The man in the moon?

Howl at the Moon
Want to hear a funny story? When we were traveling as a kid, we stopped our motorhome for the night in the middle of the desert where all these other motorhomes were parked for the night. It was warm and most people had their motorhome doors open. The moon was full. It was dusk. Quiet. And then a dog started howling. My dad, who was standing in our motorhome doorway howled at the moon along with the dog. A woman looked out her own motorhome door, a bit startled to see a grown man howling. So, he said, "Pardon me, ma'am, I was just howling at the moon."

How about you? Can you turn some heads by howling at the moon?

Family Night Walk

On a clear night you might be able to see the stars, or bump into your neighbors. If it is near Christmastime I'll bet you see some lovely Christmas lights while bonding with your family and getting exercise and fresh air.

Sparklers

Write your name in the sky with a sparkler.

Safety First: You will need an adult to light your sparkler as well as supervise you as sparklers are very hot.

Watch Fireworks

Look for Shooting Stars

According to NASA, shooting stars aren't really shooting stars. They're meteors which are bits of rock that have fallen off comets or asteroids. They are often very small (pebble sized or smaller). The reason we can see these small bits is because they're burning up as they enter the Earth's atmosphere—that's what we see. When they disappear, it is because they have burned up.

Astronomical Events

Find out when the next comet, meteor shower, or other astronomical event is coming your way. You can look up this information online or ask at your local observatory. As well, there are lots of sky maps that will tell you when the next astrological event is coming—they'll tell you when to look and what part of the sky you'll see the planet, comet, asteroid, or special something!

Make Your Own Constellation

A constellation is a group of stars that look like an animal or person, has a name and usually also has a story or legend attached to it.

Look up at the stars. Can you see a group of stars that look like something? Name your constellation and create a story about it.

WINTER PLAY

Play is our need to adapt the world to ourselves and create new learning experiences.

David Elkind
The Power of Play

You've gotta have cold or snow for these activities! And yes, we all want to stay inside where it's cozy and warm, but once you get outside and begin enjoying these activities you won't even notice the cold. It's important for kids to play outdoors all year round in order to stay healthy and active—us adults, too!

Snow Angels

Flop onto your back in the snow and wave your arms and legs up and down. Stand up and look at your angel in the snow.

Ice Sculpture

What you'll need: Plastic containers (such as margarine containers, ice cream pails, and yogurt tubs work well), water, food coloring, a squeeze bottle (an old dish detergent bottle or shampoo bottle works well).

Fill plastic containers about 3/4 full of water and add a few drops of food coloring. Freeze. Then dump them out—these are your building blocks for your sculpture.

Pour warm water into your squeeze bottle and take everything outside. Place your frozen shapes on top of each other, squeezing water (your sculpture glue) in between the pieces to make them freeze together. Have fun!

Study Snowflakes

Are all snowflakes different or can you find two the same?

Crack the Ice on Top of Mud Puddles

Another toddler and big kid favorite.

In the fall and spring, stomp on the tops of frozen mud puddles to make them crack. Wear your rubber boots! And watch the ice, it's slippery!

Safety First: Make sure the mud puddles are **not** deep because the water will be very cold! Do **NOT** do this on ponds or lakes.

More cold weather fun!

- Snowball Fight
- Drink Hot Chocolate (with marshmallows!)
- Knock the Frost and Snow off Bushes
- Winter Camping
- Sleigh Rides
- Tobogganing/Sledding
- Catch Snowflakes on Your Tongue

Tractor Tracks

Find a clear patch of snow. Using your feet, we're going to make tracks that look like tractor tires.

Place the heel of your left foot so it almost touches the arch of your right foot and step down. (Your toes point out on both feet.) Keep on going… patiently one foot after the other until you have a track that looks like one tractor tire rolled through the snow. Then about five feet from that track, make another one for the other tire. VROOOOOM!

Buy Flowers

Have the winter blues? Some nice flowers might help. You don't have to spend a lot to perk up you and your family.

Build…

- Snowmen
- Snow Chairs
- Snow Forts/Igloos
- Tunnels (*Safety First:* Dig in big, hard snowdrifts so they don't collapse in on you and ask and adult for help judging which drifts are safest.)

Snow Cats

Do you have damp, sticky snow good for making snowballs? Do you have some trees with trunks without a ton of branches, too? Then let's make snow cats!

Grab a big pile of snow and clump it together in a big ball, then smack it against a tree trunk to make a round cat's body. (We're going to make it look as though a cat (made out of snow) is clinging to the tree!) Next, take a smaller snowball and stick it to the tree just above the body. This will be the cat's head. Then, shape bits of snow for arms and legs and a nice long tail. It's a cat!

What other snow animals can you make?

Broomball

Broomball has the same rules as hockey and is played on ice. Instead of using a hockey stick and a puck, you use brooms and a ball. As well, players wear their shoes on the ice instead of skates.

Bring the Snow Indoors

Bring the snow inside! When it's too cold out for toddlers to stay out for long (or its impossible for them to move in all that gear!), fill a cake pan with clean snow and bring it inside. Let your child play with the snow in the pan. (Place a towel under it to catch any snow that falls out and melts.)

Kids will love playing with small toys in the snow—fairy figurines, toy trucks and a bulldozer… you name it! Or, simply allow them to make small snowmen as the snow gets softer and stickier. Add food coloring or glitter… get creative and have fun with this natural sensory play idea.

Get active…
- Ice-skating
- Ringette
- Hockey (You can play on ice or on the grass or on asphalt or in a basement…)
- Cross-Country Skiing
- Downhill Skiing
- Snowboarding
- Curling
- Ice Fishing
- Snowshoeing
- Snowmobiling (*Safety First:* Don't forget to wear your helmet and have an adult drive.)

PAPER CRAFTS

Play enhances the retention of knowledge and is not the enemy of learning. It is its partner.

Stuart Brown
Play

Practice fine motor skills with these paper crafts. And as with all activities in this book, make them your own. Modify and adapt them. Make them simple, make them complex. Own it!

Mini-Boomerang

You will need: thin cardboard (a cereal box is great), scissors, markers or paint.

Cut out a boomerang shape (a stretched out "U") from your cardboard. It's a boomerang!

Color or paint your boomerang.

Here's where we get to play! To fly your boomerang we're going to need a launch pad. Don't worry, a book will do. Hang one of the boomerang's ends over the edge of the book. Then tip the book up slightly—this will give your boomerang some lift. Now, flick the edge of your boomerang with your finger. Ta-da!

Did it come back to you? Did it spin a lot? Fly two at once!

Want to change the way it flies? Alter the shape of your boomerang and see if it changes the way it flies. What if you made it wider? Or longer? Or bent its edge up slightly? Experiment!

Fan

You will need: paper and a stapler.

Fold one edge of the paper up about 1 inch (2.5 cm). (If you want a longer fan, fold on the long side of the paper. If you want a shorter, wider fan, fold on the short side of the paper.)

Turn the paper over and without unfolding the fold, fold the end up in the other direction 1 inch (2.5 cm). Flip it over and repeat. Keeping flipping and folding until you have no more paper to fold. Staple one end of the fan (or wrap tape around it) to keep the folds together. Voila! You now have a fan.

Tip: Decorate your fan by painting or coloring the paper before folding it. You can also cut small pieces out of the folded fan to make it delicate and dainty.

Party Tablecloth

Having a party? Spread out a long roll of paper over the table and set out crayons for your guests. They'll love being able to draw on their tablecloth! (My husband and I did this for our wedding and still have some of the drawings people drew for us. And that was a REALLY long time ago.)

Origami
Instructions and supplies can be found in most craft stores as well as online.

Funny Magazine People
You will need: old magazines, scissors, and glue.

Cut different people out of catalogues, magazines, or newspapers. Mix and match their body parts or give them silly things like a tube of toothpaste for a body, or put a man's head on a woman who is wearing a dress.

Pinwheel
You will need: square piece of paper, pencil, ruler, pin, stick, scissors, a bead that your pin will fit through, and markers.

Color your square piece of paper. Draw a light "X" on your paper, with the X meeting in the middle of your paper, and the legs of the X starting in the paper's corners. Use your ruler to help you draw straight lines as well as mark the middle of your X with a dot.

Cut along your X lines but stop when you are a half inch from your center dot. Then turn the paper around and cut along that line from the other side, again, stopping a half inch from the center dot. You don't want to cut all the way along the whole X or your paper will fall apart. Do this for the other part of the X too.

You will now have 4 almost-triangles cut into your paper. Take the right bottom corner of one triangle and gently fold it in to the center of the paper, but without creasing the paper. Do this with all four of the triangle corners—you might need someone to help you hold them in place for you.

Now, push the pin through all four corners that have met in the center as well as the back of the paper. This will hold the pieces together.

Place the bead behind your pinwheel. You are now going to push the pin through the hole in the bead as well as the stick—the bead is between your pinwheel and stick. You may need to bend the end of the pin over so it doesn't slide out of the stick or poke anyone. If it's pretty pokey, you can cover its end with tape.

Ready to take your pinwheel for a spin? Ready? Set! Blow! Did your pinwheel turn when you blew air into its "sails?" Make some adjustments if it didn't.

Paper Stained Glass
You will need: tissue paper, black construction paper, glue, and scissors.

The black piece of construction paper will be your stained glass frame. Cut different shaped holes in the frame to make windows. Cut out tissue paper pieces that are a little bit bigger than your windows. They will be glued in behind the holes in the construction paper so you want them bigger than the holes, but not so big that they peek out of other holes, too. Gently glue the tissue paper in place.

Hang your stained glass in a window so light will shine through the tissue paper.

Snowflakes
You will need: square piece of paper and scissors.

Fold your square piece of paper in half. Then fold it in half again, but this time, the other direction so you have a square again. Fold your square at an angle so you now have a triangle. You can fold your paper one more time to make a skinnier triangle although this will be harder to cut through.

Ready? Cut small notches or holes and other neat shapes out of the folded paper. Cut through all the folded layers. The more holes you make, the more delicate your snowflake will be. When you are done, carefully unfold to see your snowflake.

Paper Chain
You will need: construction paper, scissors, tape or a stapler.

Cut straight strips of construction paper or other nice, colorful paper. Cut the strips about 1 inch (4 cm) wide and at least 6 inches (15 cm) long.

Take the first strip and gently loop one end over so it meets and overlaps the other end of the strip to form a circle. Where it overlaps, tape or staple it so it stays in a circle. Do the same thing with the next strip, but loop it through the first circle before closing it off, so that the two circles will be linked together. The third loop goes into the second loop. Keep adding loops until you have a long chain.

Paper chains can make fun decorations for parties and other events.

Collage

You will need: pictures for cutting up, glue, scissors, and paper.

Cut pictures out of an old newspaper or magazine. You can use a theme such as animals, or vacation spots, or simply things you like. Arrange and glue the pictures on another piece of paper to make a collage. The more, the better!

Fortune Square

You will need: square paper, pen, and markers. Don't forget a friend to read the fortune to!

Fold all four corners of a square piece of paper into the center so the corners just touch each other but do not overlap. You will have a square piece of paper when you're done.

Fold the new corners in one more time like you did before.

Turn the piece of paper over so your folded-in corners are face down. Now fold the new side's four corners into the middle like you did on the other side. On this side, write down eight different numbers on the four folded-in triangles (there should be a fold down the middle of each triangle–write a number on each side of the fold). On the underside of these folds write eight different fortunes or sayings about people. For example: "You look nice today," or "You will marry a rich person," or "You will sail around the world."

Flip your fortune square over and write or color four different colors on those four flaps. (These ones don't have the crease down the middle of them.)

Now put your pointer finger and thumb of each hand under each colored flap. This part is tricky, you have to fold and bend the paper so you can touch all four colored corners up together while keeping your fingers and thumbs inside the flaps.

Find a friend and ask them to pick a color. Spell out the color while moving the flaps open forwards or sideways for each letter. Then have them pick one of the numbers that shows from the inside when you are done spelling. Count out that number while opening and closing the flaps like before. Have them pick one more number from inside when you're done counting, then look underneath for their fortune!

Paper Accordion

You will need: stapler and 2 strips of paper about 1 to 2 inches wide (2.5 to 5 cm) and as long as you can make them.

Take your two strips of paper and arrange them so they form a large "L" shape. Staple the two ends together so they stay in the L shape. Fold the bottom strip over the other maintaining the L shape—the strip you just folded will be pointing the exact opposite direction that it was before you folded it. Then fold the other strip over the one you just folded. Keep alternating as you fold. On and on until the two strips are folded into a long accordion shape. Finally, staple the finished end so it can't unfold on you. Done!

Make a Hat

You will need: newspaper (or a really big sheet of plain paper) and tape.

Fold your opened newspaper sheet in half (you can use its own fold for this). Have the open edges of the fold facing you. Next, fold down the top right corner so the corner comes to the bottom middle of the page. You want the piece you are folding down to line up along the center of the paper—your corner might not reach down the bottom edge of the paper (that's perfect!). The piece you folded should be a triangle shape (but not the whole sheet of paper). Now fold down the top left corner so it meets the right corner at the bottom middle of the paper.

You should now have a shape almost like s triangle. Put a piece of tape across the two folded pieces to hold them together so they don't unfold. You now have part of a hat... sort of.

To make the hat brim, take the top piece of paper flap that falls down past the rest of the triangle. Fold it up 2-3 times and tape it to the main triangle of the hat. Flip the hat over, and fold the second flap up on that side. Open the inside of your big triangle—between the folded up flaps—and pop it on your head! You now have a hat! Looks a bit piratey doesn't it?

Your Future Home

You will need: paper, magazine pictures, scissors, and glue.

What do you dream your house will look like when you grow up? Cut pictures of things like yards and furniture out of a newspaper, magazine, or catalogue. Glue them onto a blank sheet of paper to make your future house. Can't find an idea you have? Draw it in.

Pop-Up Book

Can you make a pop-up book? This is a great craft for older kids who'd like an extra challenge. You can find instructions online or in special pop-up book books or like I enjoy doing... wing it!

Create a Placemat

You will need: paper, pens or markers.

You can make a placemat out of an ordinary piece of paper. Simply draw pictures with crayons, paints, pens or pencil crayons. You can also glue pictures or other things to your placemat.

If you laminate (sealed in plastic) your placemat at an office supply store, you can wipe it if you spill on it. Or, if you have MACtac (sticky clear plastic stuff—it's kind of like giant tape...) you can cover your picture with that to protect your placemat from spills.

Hint: Try and keep your placemat thin. If it is too thick, you won't be able to laminate it.

Paper Airplanes

There are a billion and one ways to make a paper airplane. No, really. Here's a simple one to get you started...

Take one rectangular sheet of paper and fold it down the middle lengthwise (along the long end to make it long and skinny.) Unfold your paper. Fold the top right corner down so it lines up with the paper's middle crease which you made with the first fold. Your folded down piece will form a triangle shape. Do this on the left side as well. Your two folded down pieces now will make a big triangle (if you look at just them and ignore the bottom part of the paper). Fold this whole triangle down, making the paper shorter. Fold the top, right corner down to the middle crease like you did before. Do the same with the left side. Fold your paper in half again like you did with the first fold so the triangles are on the inside of the fold.

Next are wings. Take one side and fold it down from the pointy tip, out to the end of the paper, folding down the wing so it meets and lines up with the bottom of the plane's body. (Make it flush.) Do the same on the other side. Take these folded down wing pieces and lift them up a bit until they make a flat top.

Clear the runway, you're ready to fly!

Paper Cut Outs

To make paper cut out pictures, you will need two pieces of different colored or different textured paper. Cut shapes and pieces out of the one sheet of paper and glue them over the other, uncut piece of paper. Make abstract patterns and images or arrange them like an animal or house.

OR

Cut out shapes or patterns in one piece of paper, then lay it over the other piece of paper so the other paper shows through below.

Paper Doll Chain

You will need paper, pencil, and scissors.

Fold your paper like an accordion. To do that, start on one end of your paper and fold it up about an inch and a half (4 cm). Then, flip the paper over and take your inch and a half fold and fold it (as well as the paper that is over it) up an inch and a half (4 cm). Flip your paper over and fold the fold up again. Keep going until you are at the end of your paper.

Now, draw half a person on the top fold of your folded paper. Starting on the left fold, draw half a head–the middle of the head will be right at the fold. Draw the neck and body. The arms and legs come next and will reach all the way out to the right fold. Next, cut out your body–make sure you cut through all the folds–but do not cut the folds apart. You should have folded up half a body when you're done.

Unfold. You should have a chain of people holding hands with their feet touching.

Make a Flip Book

You'll need a pencil or pen and a notebook (or build your own by cutting out 2 x 2 inch squares (5 x 5 cm) of paper and stapling them together. You're going to need *at least* 15 pages in your 'notebook' for this one). On each page (or each corner is best) draw something easy and simple such as a smiley face.

Then, on each next page/drawing make tiny changes to the face so when you flip through the notebook, watching the drawings move past, they will look like a movie with the smiley face slowly turning into something else like a frown.

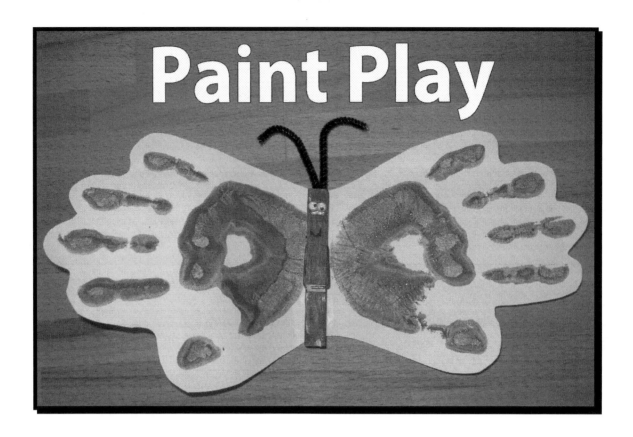

PAINT PLAY

> Children use play as therapy for dealing with stress and it can also often help them deal with impulses that are socially unacceptable.
>
> David Elkind
> The Power of Play

Ready to get messy? Grab your paint shirt! (*Hint:* An old dress shirt works well—button it up the back, roll up the sleeves, and dive on in.)

This section of the book takes your usual painting crafts outside the box—and even outside the house—in ways your kids will surely love. You might even find yourself wanting to give a few of these a try.

P.S. Toddlers LOVE the sensory experience of painting with their fingers.

Paint
Paint your own picture… paint in a paint book… paint-by-numbers…

Finger Paint
Tempra paints and other non-toxic water-based paints that are easy to wash off are great for finger painting. Use your fingers instead of a paint brush.

Paint the Sidewalk
Take powdered tempra paint and mix it with water in a paint tray. Use a paint roller to roll the paint onto the sidewalk.

Scratch Drawings
Color a piece of paper with crayons. Fill the paper with lots of small sections of dark color. Paint over it all with black tempra paint. When the paint is dry, using a toothpick, scratch a picture into the paint. The colored crayon from underneath the paint will show through giving your new picture a really neat effect.

Identical-Sided Paintings/Mirror Paintings
Paint one side of a piece of paper and while the paint is still wet, fold the paper in half and press down. The paint from the one side is now on both sides of the paper!

Drippy Paintings
Put lots of paint on your paper, then while it is still wet, hold it up over a piece of plastic (or something washable in case it drips). Let the paint run down and make interesting streaks. What happens if you turn the paper the other way? Do your drips change direction? Can you make cool effects like swirls?

Splatter Paint
Make sure your brush has lots of paint on it, then flick your brush at the paper, making splatters. (Make sure you cover your painting area with plastic—paint can end up *everywhere*!)

Feather Paintbrushes
Use a feather as a paintbrush in your paints. What else can you use? Grass? Leaves? Cotton balls? Or cotton swabs? Twigs? Pipe cleaners? What sort of lines do they make when you paint with them?

Spray Bottle Painting
You will need: a bed sheet or canvas, a spray bottle, tempera paint, warm water.

Mix your liquid tempera paint with half its amount in warm water. So if you add 1 cup (250 mL) of paint in your spray bottle, add 1/2 cup (125 mL) of warm water as well. Mix it well.

Spray away! (On your canvas or sheet.)

Painting Patterns
Using lots of paint, create swirls and blobs on a piece of paper, then while the painting is still nice and wet cover it with plastic wrap. Smooth the plastic over the paint, letting some wrinkles stay. When the paint is dry, peel off the plastic and voila! What kinds of neat patterns and effects did the plastic wrap create?

Tip: You can make beautiful homemade cards using this method—simply use watercolor paper or card stock instead of paper.

Salt Painting
What would happen if you mixed coarse salt or table salt into your wet painting? Mix it around with your fingers or paintbrush and see what happens!

Shaving Cream Paintings
Toddlers love this one!

Mix shaving cream and food coloring to make thick foamy paint. For paint brushes, try cotton swabs or old toothbrushes to smear the shaving cream paint over paper.

Hint: Use thicker paper or special painting paper from the craft store as this is wet stuff!

Safety First: Be careful your kiddos don't eat this—it looks yummy sometimes. As well, food coloring stains—wear a paint shirt and be careful they don't rub the shaving cream in their eyes.

Paint on Windows
Tempra paint comes off easily with water and a cloth. Mix it extra thick for bright, solid colors that won't run off the glass.

Tire Tracks Painting
Got washable paint? Got paper? Got toy cars?

Ready? Set? Drive! (Want more fun? Take them through the toy car wash in the Water Play section afterward.)

Variation: Dinosaurs love to paint, too. What other toys can you use to make painting something new and interesting?

Face Painting
Why let your face have all the fun? How about your hands and feet?

Artistic Play

ARTISITC PLAY

"Ironically the sheer abundance, variety, and omnipresence of toys make it harder for children to engage in truly imaginative play," says David Elkind (author of *The Power of Play*). "Battery-operated toys are attention getting and use up children's time but are of little or no developmental value." In other words, toys that have a specific purpose have very little room for imaginary play. "There is a subtle message that parents who do not buy these educational toys for their children are really not doing a good job as parents." The worst part is that these toys are designed and marketed for parental appeal, or as Elkind says so pointedly, "speak to parental fears and anxieties."

In this chapter, let it all roll off you. Follow your hearts, your imaginations, and your creative spirit and see where it takes you with these crafts. Enjoy leaving those store-bought toys in the toy box (okay, they're probably strewn all over the house for a real-life obstacle course if your home is anything like mine) and make your own play items. There is something satisfying about making a craft that can be played with in any way you and your child desire. Your kids are into superheroes? No problem, their fist puppet can be one of those! And when they draw on the newspaper, they can give everyone capes and masks. Run with it!

Fist Puppets
Make a fist (with your thumb touching the knuckle on your pointer finger). Your thumb will be the bottom lip and chin of the puppet. The top knuckle of your pointer finger will be the top of the puppet's head. You can make a face with pens or markers—just make sure they are the kind that wash off!

Imprints
Place a coin (you can also use a leaf or other thin, bumpy object) under a piece of paper. Gently color the paper over the coin with a crayon or pencil. Watch as the impression (bumps) of the coin magically appear in your coloring!

What else can you make an imprint of?

Draw On the Newspaper
Give people moustaches, horns, funny thought bubbles, etc. Make sure your parents are done with the newspaper first! (You can also use magazines.)

Blind Contour Drawings
Draw a picture of something without looking at the paper you are drawing on. Pick something that will stay still, like a chair or a plant. Without looking at the paper, draw the object. No cheating!

Don't Lift Your Pencil
Draw a picture of something without lifting your pencil off the paper. Find something you want to draw and start drawing. Once you place your pencil on the paper, do not lift it again until you're done your entire drawing.

Double Drawing

Take two pencils, pencil crayons, or pens and tape them together (or use a rubber band) so they're stuck together. Draw a picture or write something as you normally would, but instead of making one line you will be making two. A double drawing! Does it look strange?

Charcoal Drawings

Drawing charcoal is available at most art supply stores.

Hint: Check out how to make your own charcoal pen in the Mother Earth Outdoor Play section—adult assistance is required for that activity.

Pastels

Pastels are available in arts and craft stores and are great for making bright, colorful drawings.

Profiles

You will need: a friend, paper, tape, pencil, dark room, and a lamp.

Make a room dark, except for the light from your lamp (take the shade off to create better shadows). Have your friend stand or sit close to the wall so the lamp creates their shadow on the wall. You might have to adjust where the lamp sits and where your friend is.

Tape the piece of paper to the wall where your friend's shadow is.

Turn your friend so they create a side profile shadow. That means in their wall shadow you can see their forehead, nose, lips, and chin. (Your friend is not facing the paper or the lamp.)

Once you have them standing in the right place, trace the outline of their profile onto the paper. Ta-da! Does it look like them?

Trace Your Hands or Feet

Place your hand or foot on a piece of paper and draw around it with a pencil to make an outline of your foot. Bet it tickles!

Trace your Body

Why stop with your hands or feet?

Trace a Picture

Place a blank piece of paper over the picture you want to trace, then hold both up against a window so light shows through both papers, making it easier to see the lines you are going to trace.

Body Outline

Boy, I'm tired. Time to lay down on the sidewalk, in the sand, packed snow or maybe on a large piece of paper and have a little nap. Oh! What's this? Someone is tracing the outline of my body onto the ground! Oh, would you look at that? They made it look like I was running!

Aluminum Tracing

You will need: A thin piece of aluminum, tape, a picture you want to trace (make an impression of on the aluminum), a newspaper, and a pencil.

Place your sheet of aluminum over a newspaper to give it some cushion behind it. Then, take your tracing photo and place it over top. Tape it to the aluminum so it doesn't move on you. Go over all of the photo's lines by pressing your pencil evenly while tracing. This will dent the aluminum and 'transfer' what you draw onto the aluminum!

Variation: Try it with aluminum foil.

Hint: You don't have to have a photo to trace. You can place a blank piece of paper over your aluminum and simply draw a picture which will then dent the aluminum—making a copy!

How about this...
- Color in a Coloring Book
- Draw a Picture
- Color or Paint one of Your Drawings
- Illustrate (draw pictures for) your Favorite Story

Calligraphy

Hint: You can find books on calligraphy, plus calligraphy pens in an arts and crafts store.

Draw Caricatures of Your Friends

A caricature is a goofy cartoon drawing that looks like someone.

Draw on Eggs

When I was a kid I'd take hard boiled eggs in my lunch. To show that they were hard boiled, my mom would draw faces on them. (So I wouldn't take raw eggs by mistake!) When I'd crack them open at school, the boy sitting next to me would always shout (as though he was the egg), "Oh! My head!"

Hint: Pencils work well.

Fluffy Snowman

Draw three circles on a piece of paper to make a snowman's body. Then with glue, stick cotton balls in the circles to make a fluffy snowman! Cut a hat out of black construction paper or felt or simply draw one on. Get creative with buttons, arms, and a face for your snowman.

Popcorn Pictures

Pop some unsalted, unbuttered popcorn and get creative! Grab your glue, paper, markers… even paint. Glue the popcorn on your paper to make fluffy popcorn trees, dogs, cats, T. Rexes and more! Your imagination is the limit.

Star Gazer

You will need: black construction paper, pin, tape, Styrofoam cup, and a pen.
Tape the paper over the mouth of the Styrofoam cup. Punch a small hole in the bottom of the cup using the pen. Then using the pin, punch tiny holes (stars) in the black paper.

Look through the hole in the bottom of the cup. Do you see the stars you made?

Paperweight

A paperweight is a nice object that is heavy enough to hold papers on a desk so they won't blow off if there is a breeze.

A nice rock can make a good paperweight. Want to dress it up? Paint it! Glue interesting things to it. Ta-da!

Pick a Project

Go to the craft section at your local store, or go to a store devoted just to crafts. Look around for your next project. What jumps out at you and looks like fun? Try it out! There's something for everyone.

Rain Stick
A preschooler favorite!

You will need: empty paper towel tube, aluminum foil, 1/4 cup (60 mL) rice, glue, and stickers.

Take a small square of aluminum foil and glue it over one end of your paper towel roll. Make sure it is smooth.

Next, we are going to make something for inside the tube so the rice (rain) has something to fall against so it doesn't just plunk from side to side in the rain stick, but actually sounds a bit like rain when the stick is turned over. Take a long piece of aluminum foil (about two times longer than the paper towel roll—about 2 feet (60 cm). Fold this piece in half lengthwise (fold to make it skinnier, not shorter), then gently scrunch it into a long strand—but not super tight. We're now going to stuff it in the paper towel roll. It's going to be too long which is perfect, we want a few bends in it for the rice to get caught on as it moves through the tube.

Now, pour the rice into the tube. You can already hear it falling through the scrunched up strand like rain! (Don't fill the tube completely as your rice will need room to move and fall.)

Finally, take a small square of aluminum foil and cover the open end of the roll. Glue the end in place. Time to decorate! Take another piece of aluminum foil and cover the outside of the towel roll. (You could also paint it, cover it with wrapping paper, or whatever suits your fancy.) Glue the outside foil in place and decorate with stickers, ribbons, or whatever you like. Make it yours.

Let's try it out! When you slowly turn your rain stick over the rice will fall from one end to another, hitting your scrunched up aluminum foil as it goes and creating a cool rain-like sound. I think we need a rain dance to go with this craft!

Make a Calendar
Print your own at home using an online template or a template in your word processing software. Use photographs of your family, pets, or friends to personalize the calendar. Print it off at home, or send it to a stationary or print shop and they can print it and bind it just like a real calendar. These make great gifts!

Binoculars

You will need: 2 toilet paper rolls, string/yarn, glue, pencil or a single hole punch. For decoration, you might like items such as tinfoil or foil from a chocolate bar wrapper, wrapping paper, pictures from a magazine, paint, markers, or stickers.

Take two empty toilet paper rolls and glue them together (side to side).

Next we'll add a strap so they can hang around your neck. (This is optional. If your kids are small, you might not want to add a strap due to safety concerns.) Punch a small hole on the left side and the right side of the binoculars (near one end). To make a strap, pull a piece of string or yarn (about 15 inches long (40 cm)) through the holes and tie each end in place with a knot.

Ready? Let's decorate your binoculars. You can make them shiny by covering them with tinfoil or foil from chocolate bars. (Sorry, going to have to eat that chocolate bar first. Shucks!) Add stickers. Paint them. Whatever suits your fancy.

Hint: This is a great accessory to go with your cardboard box submarine (found in the Construction Crafts section).

Spyglass

You will need: one paper towel roll, glue, and decorations such as tinfoil or foil from a chocolate bar wrapper, wrapping paper, pictures from a magazine, paint, markers, or stickers.

Paint or decorate the outside of the paper towel roll. Ta-da! What do you see? Pirates? Asteroids? Someone coming up to your treehouse?

Hint: This is a great accessory to go with your cardboard box submarine (found in the Construction Crafts section).

Centerpiece

A centerpiece is something you place in the middle of a table for decoration. There are hundreds upon hundreds of different ideas when it comes to centerpieces. What do you think would look nice? Something made of flowers? Pinecones? Wood? Paper? Be creative.

Hint: If you need ideas or designs, try craft books at your local library.

Place Setting Name Tags for the Table

Postcard
Cut out a piece of cardstock (poster paper) so it is 4 x 6 inches (10 x 15 cm). (If you mail it, you won't have to add extra postage for this size.)

Decorate the postcard however you desire. Glue a photo or other picture(s) onto the postcard or draw your own. Write on the back, add a stamp and mail it away!

Homemade Cards

Memory Box
A memory box is a decorated box for storing special items. Usually they are made to remember a person or a special event. For example, if you went on a vacation, or a friend was moving away, you might make a memory box for that trip or that person.

You will need: a small box with a lid (like a shoebox), mementoes, glue or tape, ribbon, photos, glitter, stickers and other things you would like to use to decorate your box.

Decorate both the inside and outside of the box. You can glue your mementos (special items like pictures, ticket stubs and postcards) onto the box or simply place them inside.

Paper Flowers
You will need: tissue paper and pipe cleaners.

Take 4-6 rectangular pieces of tissue paper. Stack the sheets on top of each other and fold them together like you're making a paper fan (see the fan craft in the Paper Crafts section). Only—don't staple the end of the tissue paper when you're done folding. Make 5 folds by folding the sheets along the long side of the rectangle—you want a long folded strip when you're done. Wrap a piece of pipe cleaner around the middle of the tissue paper accordion. Gently pull each layer of tissue paper upwards on both sides of the accordion to make it shaped like the bloom of a flower. Twist another pipe cleaner onto the one wrapped around the tissue paper to make a stem, then twist onto the stem a few pipe cleaners bent into leaf shapes.

Pipe Cleaner Animals
Bend pipe cleaners into different animal shapes. Can you create a whole zoo of animals?

Make your own...
- Homemade Paper
- Book
- Bookmark
- Photo Album
- Scrapbook
- Candles
- Board Game
- Sew Something
- Knit/Crochet
- Dreamcatcher
- Paint a Flower Pot

Puzzle

All you need is a picture from a magazine or an old postcard or photo that can be cut up. You'll also need scissors, glue and thin cardboard such as a cereal box.

To make your puzzle stronger, glue your puzzle magazine picture/postcard/photo to an old cereal box before cutting it out into puzzle shapes. Cut your picture into different shapes and sizes, then try to put it back together!

Decorate a Mug

There are lots of ways to decorate a mug. There are studios where you can paint cups and other dishes, or you can buy special paints so you can do it at home, or you can go online and upload your own photos to a photo department at your local store and have them place it on a cup for you.

Carve Soap

Draw a pattern (where you want to cut) onto the soap before you start. Take a small knife or carving tool and cut out your design.

Safety First: Be very careful! Always cut away from yourself and use lots of small cuts in the soap instead of bigger cuts. As well, talk to an adult first to ensure you have the proper supplies and that your parents feel you are old enough to tackle this craft.

Hint: Try soft bars of soap and a plastic knife.

Decorate a Picture Frame

This is a great gift idea and often you can find cheap frames at dollar stores or garage sales. If you're feeling extra creative you can try making your own out of cardboard.

Some decoration ideas to jumpstart your project: Paint your frame or cover it with cloth or puzzle pieces. Glue items like small photos, bits of fabric, string, beads, ribbon, or stick stickers and other fun and interesting things to the picture frame. Can you decorate it in a theme that matches the photo you plan to put inside?

Magnets

There are many different ways to make your own magnets. If you're good with computers and have a printer, you can buy magnet sheets at stationary stores which you can print onto directly. This is nice if you like to make drawings on the computer or if you have digital pictures you would like to have on magnets. Simply, print, cut, stick to metal. Boom! You're done.

If you want to get a bit more crafty, re-cover old magnets or buy magnets you can add things to in the store. Glue pictures, drawings, funny sayings, feathers, and well, just about anything onto the magnet.

Hint: If you put too many things on the magnet it might get too heavy to stick your fridge! Oops.

Decorate a Shirt

Decorate a plain shirt with permanent fabric markers, fabric paints, or iron-on applications. (Most computer or stationary stores carry iron-on print out sheets. Take designs or pictures off your computer, print them onto the special paper and iron them onto your shirt.)

Doll Parachutes

Does your doll want to fly? Let's give her a parachute. (Small, light dolls work best.) Plastic grocery bags with its handles looped around the doll's arms or tied with string can make a fast and easy parachute.

Safety First: Don't let small children play with plastic bags as they are a suffocation hazard.

Tie Dye

Safety First: Have an adult help you with this one.

You will need: clothing for dying, dye, water, buckets, rubber bands or thick string, and rubber gloves.

Find an item of clothing (something white is best) that is okay to dye a different color. If your item is brand new, wash and dry it before tie-dying.

Tie strips of cloth around the item you are dying. Where you tie the strips the dye won't color the material bunched underneath and it will remain its original color. Make sure the ties are very tight so dye doesn't seep all the way underneath.

Have an adult mix your dye according to the dye's package directions. If you mix the dye in a large bucket you can easily dip your item into the dye. Make sure you wear old clothes, rubber gloves (so you don't dye your hands), and cover your work area with plastic or newspaper. After dipping the item in the dye a few times, rinse it really well in cold water and then again in warm water. After rinsing, take off the ties and admire your new tie-dyed item. (Lay flat to dry.)

Old Looking Paper

Stain plain white paper with tea to make it look aged! This is great for history assignments.

Drag a warm, wet tea bag over your paper, or place the paper in a tray of ready-made tea. (Iced tea mix or coffee will also work.) Your paper, once wet, will want to curl as it dries. Smooth the paper over a board and staple it in place. It will dry flat as it won't be able to curl.

And there you have it! Paper that looks super old! (You can also rip the edges a bit to make it look worn.)

Macramé

Macramé is like knitting and crocheting, only you make knots instead of weaving the yarn. There are lots of different projects, designs, and types of knots. Go to a craft store and look at project ideas and materials, or if you know someone who does macramé, get them to show you how. They may even let you use some of their supplies. Or simply just start knotting yarn and see where it takes you!

Weave

Weave your shoelaces, a bracelet, a grass basket, mini elastic bands, or a wall hanging. What can you make?

Beading

Project ideas: Make jewelry, key chains, bags, people or animals, bookmarks... Weave your beads! String your beads!

Yarn Bombing

Have yarn? Want to have some fun? Yarn bombing is when you take yarn and weave or wrap it around something in nature like a tree, fence, or stop sign post. Make it pretty! Don't forget to go back and take it down in a few weeks.

Popcorn String

You will need: popcorn, needle, and string.

Pop popcorn in an air popper (do not use microwave popcorn unless it is salt-free and butter-free—in other words natural and plain). Thread a needle with string and stick the needle through the popcorn. Keeping sewing popcorn onto your string until you have the length you want. You can place it on the Christmas tree or decorate an outdoor tree so animals can snack on it.

Friendship Bracelets

Got a friend? Make them a friendship bracelet. Typically, friendship bracelets are made by knotting and weaving several strands of embroidery thread, but you can use whatever your heart desires. Make them matching—one for your friend, one for yourself.

Melt Crayons

You will need: crayons, iron, wax paper, newspaper, and an adult's help.

Peel the paper wrapper off a few crayons. Make shavings by scraping the crayon with a butter knife. Place the shavings between two sheets of wax paper. Arrange them to make a picture or something abstract. Place a piece of newspaper over top and underneath the wax paper so it doesn't stick to the iron or your ironing board.

Safety First: Have an adult put your iron on the lowest setting and slowly iron over the newspaper until the crayon bits between the wax paper melts—don't leave it in one spot for too long! How does it look? Careful—it's hot!

Jewelry
There are lots of different ways to make your own jewelry.

Supply ideas: String, wire, fishing line, beads, shells, buttons, uncooked noodles or Cheerios.

Rock Animals
Did you find a rock that has a shape like an animal? Or maybe it's just a round stone that would make a great head or body for a new animal creation.

What shall we do? How about paint a face on it. (You can also use markers.) If you have googly eyes, you can glue those on for eyes. It almost looks like a mouse? Add a string tail and some big round ears. Or maybe it looks like it needs a cotton ball tail… How about some legs? Get creative!

Tissue Paper Jar
You will need: empty jar or can about 3 - 4 inches tall (8 - 10 cm) with a wide opening at the top, tissue paper, pencil, white glue, and a shallow container for glue (like a jar lid).

Cut different colored tissue paper into small squares (1 x 1 inch (3 x 3 cm)).

Gently wrap one square of tissue paper over the eraser end of a pencil. Lightly dip it in glue so the middle of the tissue paper is covered with glue. Stick the gluey part of the tissue paper onto the jar or can. The center of the tissue paper should stick to the jar while the rest of the square pokes out, away from the jar. Continue until the jar is covered, placing your squares close together.

Variation: For younger kids or ones with a bit less patience, completely cover one side of the jar with glue (paintbrushes work well for spreading the glue) then lay the tissue paper squares flat over the surface of the jar. It will be smooth and fast—and that appeals to speed crafters who don't like finicky.

Now, doesn't that look lovely? What shall we do with it? You can use it as a pencil jar for holding pencils on your desk or place a battery operated tea light under the upside down jar and see what colors glow!

Make a Headdress

A headdress is a type of ceremonial hat. You can make one similar to the traditional Native American headdress with feathers attached to a beaded band. Or, you can make one out of paper and color it with markers. Be creative!

Decorate a Hat

Decorate a hat you already have or make your own using the instructions for making a paper hat found in the Paper Crafts section. Depending on the hat, you can paint it, color it, sew things onto it, add stickers, tape pictures to it, glue feathers, beads or flowers, or even make a whole new crazy hat of your own by shaping aluminum foil around your noggin! Your imagination is the limit.

Toilet Paper Roll Animals

Using a toilet paper roll for a body, add feet, faces, ears, tails… whatever your animal needs! Get creative and use whatever crafting supplies you have on hand. Want a cat? How about a yarn tail? Rabbit? Add a cotton ball tail. Pig? Twisted pipe cleaner for a tail.

Mask

You will need: paper plate (or a piece of flexible, round cardboard that has an unmarked side), string, markers (crayons, paints, or pencil crayons), and scissors.

Draw a face on your paper plate mask with markers, crayons, pencil crayons or paint. Ask an adult to cut out the eye holes and two tiny holes at the sides by the ears. Thread a piece of string through the side holes and adjust it to make the mask fit your head.

What kind of mask are you making? Is it a cat? Add whiskers and ears. An elephant? Add a trunk.

Variations: Instead of drawing on the plate, glue things such as pipe cleaners, string or strips of construction paper to make facial features. Felt or fleece can make large elephant ears, fuzzy fur or a little, fuzzy, soft nose.

Is the string falling off your child's head? Glue a popsicle stick at the base of the paper plate as a handle your child can use to hold the mask in front of their face.

Butterfly

This is an easy craft for all ages, always turns out well, and is fun!

You will need: a white round paper coffee filter, washable markers, a black pipe cleaner, scissors, a spray bottle that can mist water, and two pieces of paper towel.

Cut your pipe cleaner in half and set it aside.

Color your coffee filter with washable markers. You don't need to cover the whole surface.

Hold the colored filter over the paper towel (to catch any drips that might happen) and mist the filter with water (using the spray bottle). Make sure you get the whole filter wet (but not soaked). The marker's color should be a bit runny.

While it is all still wet, carefully make one twist in the middle of the filter. This makes it suddenly look like it has two wings. Wrap your pipe cleaner around the middle of your filter (the twist). Leave the two ends of the pipe cleaner sticking up to look like antenna.

Lay the butterfly flat on a dry piece of paper towel. In about an hour, it should be dry.

Variation: Glue a magnet to the back of the butterfly to make it a magnet or tie fishing line to it and hang it from a window, or the ceiling as a decoration. You can also fold the filter into a flower shape, using pipe cleaners as a stem, such as pictured at the beginning of this chapter.

Put on an Art Show

Don't know what to do with all of your lovely new artistic creations? Put on an art show for your family and friends.

Painter's tape is typically gentle on paper *and* walls and can be used to hang your artwork for display. Or, if you can tack string along the wall, use clothespins to clip your paintings to the string. As well, setting up cardboard boxes as display tables can work well for non-hangable art. (I used to create my own museums this way so I could display my rock collection.)

Hint: You can also sell your artwork at a lemonade stand (found in the Outside Play section) or yard sale.

Light Switch Cover

Hmmm… does your room need a little decorating? An easy way to brighten up your room is to dress up your light switch cover (the rectangle plate around your light switch).

Safety First: An easy way to get the right size and shape for your light switch cover is to have an **adult** remove the cover from the wall so you can trace the shape and switch hole onto your crafting foam or special paper you will be using as a background.

Cut out your cover. Ready? Set! Decorate! Stickers. Foam stickies. Ribbons. Photos. Sequins. Sparkles and glitter. Beads. Draw. Paint… go wild!

Stick your new cover over your old plastic cover using tape (or if you are allowed, use glue). Boom! Your room looks *goooooood.*

Paper Bird Nest

You will need: Plastic or Styrofoam bowl, plastic wrap, strips of paper (long enough to hang over the sides of the bowl when laid across the bowl's inner bottom—make the strips thin (1/2 inch at most or 2-3 cm), white glue, water, container for mixing glue and water, paint brush.

Place a layer of plastic over your bowl. The bowl will shape your nest and the plastic will keep it from sticking to your bowl.

Next, take your strips of paper and layer them in the bowl with the ends sticking up, over the edges of the bowl. Mix a bit of water in a container along with the glue—you don't want it super runny, just easily spreadable. With your paint brush, brush glue over the first layer of strips, bonding them together. Keep adding layers of paper and layers of glue until you feel it is the way you want it. (You want at least 3-4 layers so the nest won't break easily.)

Allow it to dry—a day or two depending on how many layers you have. Once dry, pop it out of the bowl and peel the plastic wrap off the underside of your nest. It should hold it's nest shape. Do you have any eggs to put inside?

Make a Dog Toy

Take an old, clean sock—the bigger the better. Stuff the sock full of clean, old material like odd socks or rags. Tie a knot in the end of the sock so the stuffing doesn't come out and you're ready to play a few games like tug-o-war and fetch with your dog.

Make a Cat Toy

Cats love to chase and play with toys. Here are a few easy ones you can make at home that my own cats have enjoyed.

Dangle Toy: Take a scrap piece of material like an old sock and cut out a small strip (about 6 x 1 ½ inches wide (15 cm long x 5 cm wide). Tie this strip onto the end of a tough piece of string or yarn. Make the string about two times as long as your arm. Voila! Your cat toy is ready to be dragged slowly in front of your cat. I bet they pounce!

Variation: Instead of a strip of cloth, you can tie feathers or an existing cat toy such as a toy mouse onto the end of the string.

Catnip Toy: Stuff catnip into the toe of an old, clean sock. Above the catnip pouch, tightly tie the sock into a knot or tie it off with a piece of ribbon or string so the catnip doesn't fall out. Then above your knot or string, snip off the extra bit of sock. Set the new toy down for your cat and watch it go crazy!

CONSTRUCTION CRAFTS

> Play is not a luxury but rather a crucial dynamic of healthy physical, intellectual, and social-emotional development at all age levels.
>
> David Elkind
> The Power of Play

Nate Jones of NPL discovered that "those who had worked and played with their hands as they were growing up were able to "see solutions" that those who hadn't worked with their hands could not." How about that? All the more reason to work with your hands as a kid and figure things out.

Note: These projects may need special supplies as well as help from an adult. Large projects can make a great family activity.

Grass Head
(Pictured on previous page.)
This is a fun and easy one! Made a head where grass grows out the top!

You will need:
1 knee-high stocking (or a leg cut off of a pair of nylons)
1 tablespoon (15 mL) grass seed
3 cups (750 mL) sawdust or peat moss
bowl
saucer or plate
water
markers
white glue
wiggly eyes

Place grass seed in the toe of the stocking. Fill the foot of the stocking with sawdust or peat moss. Add enough to form a nice round "head." Make sure you don't mix the grass seed into the stocking too much or your grass head will have grass growing out his nose! Tie a knot in the stocking right above the sawdust/peat moss. You may have to squeeze the material down to make a tight, round ball. Soak your grass head in a bowl of water for 2-3 minutes or until it is heavy with water, then place it on a saucer or plate so it doesn't drip everywhere.

After a day or two, the head should be dried out enough that a face can be created. Glue on wiggly eyes, a string mouth, or draw it all with permanent markers.

Maintenance: Keep your grass head on a plate or saucer and in the sun, but don't let him get too dry. To keep him damp, dip the top of his head (the toe of the stocking where the seeds are) in water every day. In about a week, hair (grass) should start sprouting. Once it starts growing you can give him funky haircuts!

Rain Gauge
A rain gauge measures the amount of rain that falls.

You will need: a wide mouth jar, a short plastic ruler, and waterproof tape.

Place the ruler inside the jar. Tape the ruler to the jar's side so the ruler's 0 end touches the jar's bottom. Put your gauge outside when it rains so it can collect rain. When it is done raining, measure how much fell in your gauge. (You can do this with snow too.)

Hint: For best results, place your gauge away from trees and buildings so the rain can fall into your jar and isn't sheltered.

Kite
Kites can be fussy. If you don't have a good design, it won't fly right. There are lots of different kite designs and materials from simple to fancy. Look for designs in library books and on the internet. But then again... sometimes it's just fun making it and hanging it on your wall as decoration.

Toothpick Cabin
Stack toothpicks to build a cabin. Glue them together or not? Hmm... If you don't glue them, you can take it apart and build something else later.

Walking Stick
Selecting your walking stick: Look for a stick that is a bit higher than your waist when it is touching the ground. This way you can reach forward with your walking stick without having to hunch over as you walk. The stick needs to be skinny enough you can comfortably wrap your hand around it, but strong and straight enough that it doesn't bend or break if you lean on it. Tip: Pulling branches off of living trees hurts them.

Once you have a good stick, remove the little twigs or leaves off the main, long stick. You can use your walking stick the way it is, or put more work into it. If you want to make it smoother, sand it with sandpaper. To make it shiny, coat it with a layer or two of polyurethane (available at paint and hardware stores). Decorate your stick with bells, ribbons, or wrap yarn around your handle for an extra cushiony grip.

Looks like it's time go for a family hike and try out this new walking stick!

Homemade Sailboat
There are many places to float your boat: in a bathtub, mud puddle, pond, river, or lake.

Safety First: Remember to play safe around water and to always follow your family's rules about water safety. If you are floating your boat in something larger than a mud puddle, you might want to tie a string to it so it doesn't float too far away.

Hint: Need extra help getting ideas? Find plans or boat-building kits in hardware stores, arts and craft stores, online or in a boat-building book.

Paper Maché
There are many things you can make out of paper maché (animals, shapes, piñatas (see the next project following this one)). In fact, just about anything you can think of! Decide what you would like to make and prepare a structure out of wire, cardboard, or even a balloon. This will give your paper maché its shape as you layer your paper maché strips over top.

You will need:
strips of newspaper about 1 inch wide (3 cm) and strips of white paper for the last layer
bucket and spoon
mold to build onto with your paper maché (such as a balloon, cardboard, or wire structure)
1 cup (250 mL) flour
2 tablespoons (30 mL) salt
1 cup (250 mL) warm water
 Mix together: flour, salt, and warm water. Stir.

Place plastic or newspaper down where you are going to work. Dip your newspaper strips into the mix and wipe the extra mixture off by running the strip between your fingers. Place about 4 layers of strips on your structure. Allow the layers to dry (this may take hours or days) before adding 4 more layers.

Keep adding layers until you have the shape and strength you need. With the last layer, use white paper (or paper towel) instead of newspaper strips. When it is dry, paint and decorate it.

Hint: If you have to wait for layers to dry, but still have mix left, seal it with plastic wrap. Stir it before reusing it. It may turn light brown, but it will still work.

Piñata

Make a piñata out of paper maché (see above project) and fill its hollow center with candy or other treats to break open at a birthday party.

To make a hollow center, create your piñata using a balloon for its structure. Once you have dried two layers over the balloon, cut a small hole in the bottom of the piñata. Pop the balloon and fill your piñata with treats. Place the piece that was cut out of the piñata back over the hole and tape or paper maché it back into place. Add more paper maché layers. Then attach a loop of yarn to the top of your piñata when you are adding layers so you will be able to hang your piñata. Make sure you get the yarn in there tight—you might want to wrap it all the way around your piñata if it is going to be a heavy one.

Once your piñata is dry, paint it or decorate it to your heart's desire. Then invite friends over to take turns hitting it with a stick. When it breaks, the goodies will go everywhere. Goody fest!

Clay Recipe
You will need:
1 cup (250 mL) flour
1/3 cup (75 mL) warm water
1/4 cup (60 mL) salt
bowl
spoon
baking sheet
food coloring (for colored clay)

Mix the ingredients. (If the dough is too dry add more water.)

Create your masterpiece out of the clay. (Handprints are fun and easy!)

Safety First: Have an adult bake your creation at 150 F (65 C) for 1-2 hours on a cookie sheet.

Let the oven dry out the clay completely. Once it has cooled, paint it.

Tree Swing
Oh, yeah. You know what I'm talking about here. What's childhood without a tire or board swing hanging from a tree?

Plaster Molds

To make plaster, follow the directions listed on the box or bag of plaster. Pour the plaster into pre-made molds (found in arts and crafts stores) or create your own (I like ice cream pails to make a nice circle or plate). You can add things to your plaster before it sets—push a handprint into the surface of the plaster or place glass beads or other items in the surface so they peek out but will be stuck in place when the plaster hardens.

When the plaster is dry, pop it out of its mold. Want to paint your creation? Carve into it? (Plaster is fairly soft and easy to carve into. Give it a whirl!)

Hint: You can find paintable, pre-made plaster molded items (or porcelain) in arts and crafts stores if you want to skip the mixing and molding step.

Paper Bag Puppets

Take a paper lunch bag and where the bottom of the bag folds, create a face. The fold will be the puppet's mouth. Decorate your puppet by coloring, drawing, painting, or gluing things to the bag to give your puppet character as well as face.

Sock Puppets

Take an old sock that you can fit your hand into. The toe of the sock will be the mouth and nose area of the puppet. Glue or sew scrap material to the sock to make a mouth, nose, and eyes. Buttons make great eyes, and yarn or string makes excellent hair.

Finger Puppets

Take a piece of thin cardboard and cut it out into the shape of a person or an animal—but make its butt bigger (yes, really—it has to be at least wider than your pointer and middle finger squeezed together as we're going to make a hole to squeeze your finger through as your fingers will be the puppet's legs). (Don't give your puppet cardboard legs, either.)

Got your big bottomed puppet? Next, cut two holes in the bottom of the puppet for your pointer and middle fingers to fit through. (Legs.)

Give your puppet a face, outfit, etc.

Hint: Having troubles? You can find lots of free printable templates online. Search for: finger puppet templates.

Puppet Theatre

You will need: a large, narrow cardboard box, tape, scissors, fabric, and paint or crayons.

Tape the cardboard box closed. Have an adult cut a hole in the stage's front (the box's long side) where your audience will look in. Also cut a hole in the back—this is where you will hold up your puppets. The front of the theatre can be decorated with paint or crayons and staple fabric inside the top of the front to make stage curtains.

Ready? Make puppets using the ideas just above this activity and put on a play! Not sure what the play should be about? You can write your own story, reenact a fairy tale or nursery rhyme or even a family event!

Tip: Looking for a super-fast and easy puppet theatre? Sit behind the couch, pop your puppets up over the edge of the couch and put on your play! You'll be hidden behind the couch and all your audience will see are your puppets popping over the top of the couch! Easy-peasy.

Raft

Glue popsicle sticks together to make a miniature bathtub toy raft. If you have the supplies and adult help, you can make one big enough for you to ride on.

Safety First: Don't forget your lifejacket and a paddle!

Tip: A popsicle raft can be a great edition to the volcano game (found under "Volcano" in the Mad Scientist's Ooey Gooey Laboratory section! (This activity has been a tried-and-true toddler favorite in our household.)

Box Car/Truck/Submarine

Using a cardboard box, build yourself a vehicle (a car, truck, submarine, spaceship, or something else). For a larger vehicle, tape two boxes together or use a large fridge box.

To make your box look like the vehicle you want, draw or paint the outside. Paper plates make a good steering wheel and wheels. Smaller plates or muffin papers glued on the outside make great headlights. Draw a speedometer and gauges inside the box.

For smaller vehicles, cut leg holes in the bottom of the box so you can walk and staple straps onto your vehicle to help hold it up over your shoulders.
Safety First: Ask an adult to do any cutting for you.

Mobile

You will need: 3 drinking straws, fishing line (string or strong thread), 1 piece of white paper, tape, scissors, and glue.

Cut out 4 different shapes from the paper and decorate them—these can be anything you want (ex. stars, snowflakes, random shapes). These are going to dangle from your mobile. Don't make them too heavy though or your drinking straws will collapse in protest.

Take one straw (we'll call it "Alice"). You want to cut poor Alice so she's about 9.5 inches long (24 cm). Tie a piece of string that is about 6 inches long (15 cm) around Alice's middle. This will be the string for hanging your mobile from the ceiling.

Next, take Alice and tie a piece of string to each of her ends. Make one of these strings about 4 inches long (10 cm) and the other one about 10 inches long (25 cm). They are going to try and escape because Alice isn't very grippy. Tape each string to her so they don't slide off. She'd thank you for that if she could talk.

Ready for the next step? Take two straws (we'll call these Bob and Carrie), and cut them so they are about 6 inches long (15 cm). Remember those strings we just tied and taped to Alice's two ends? We're going to attach Bob and Carrie to those strings. Tie 'em on and tape 'em!

Now Bob and Carrie are going to get strings, too! For this you'll need 4 different strings that are about 6 inches long (15 cm). Got them? Tie one to each end of Bob but don't tape them in place quite yet. (One string on each of his two ends.) Now do the same to Carrie.

Time to add your shapes to make it a mobile! Grab your four shapes and tape them to the ends of Bob and Carrie's strings. They might hang a bit wonky at first and throw the whole balance of your mobile off, but that's easy to fix. While holding your mobile up by the string around Alice's middle, slide the strings with the shapes on them back and forth until you can get your mobile to balance the way you like it. Once everything is exactly where you'd like it, tape those strings (Bob and Carrie's) in place. (You might need an extra set of hands to hold the mobile while you make adjustments.)

You're done!

Variation: Use pictures from old cards, colorful foam pieces or other interesting items to hang from your mobile.

Tin Can Shoes

You will need: 2 large coffee or tomato cans, 2 pieces of long, tough string or cord (over 3 feet (1 meter) long for each can), something sharp to make holes in the cans (a nail carefully hammered through the can works well), and an adult to help you out.

Safety First: Have an adult make one small hole on either side of one can. (Two holes per can, one across the can from the other.) Make the holes as close to the can's bottom as possible.

Thread one long string through the holes and tie the ends together, making a large loop. The string's loop needs to be long enough that you can comfortably hold onto it while standing on the can.

Do the same for the other can.

Turn the cans upside down and carefully place your feet on the can bottoms. Hold onto the strings and pull up lightly to keep the cans tight to your feet as you walk. Start by taking very small steps and keep your feet close together. These shoes sound great on sidewalks. There you go! Don't you feel tall?

Hint: Tin can shoes can be difficult to use on plush carpet.

Tin Can Phone

Hello? Can you hear me? How about now?

A tree fort or sleepover just isn't the same without a tin can phone. How do you make one? Easy! All you need are two tin cans and a long piece of string. You'll also need an adult to help as well as a nail and hammer.

Safety First: Have an adult tap one hole into the bottom of each can using the nail and hammer. (If you have a power drill and a masonry bit that can work nicely, too.) You don't need a big hole—just big enough to thread string through. Watch the can when making your hole—the nail may try to slip away instead of going through the can.

More Safety: If the can's edges are sharp, place thick tape (such as duct tape) over any sharp edges to protect your children's hands.

Got your holes? (That was either easy or epic, wasn't it?) Next, thread string into the hole and tie a knot on the inside of the can so the string can't slip out. If the knot keeps slipping through the hole, tie the string to a bead or washer so it can't slide back through the can's hole. Do the same with the other can.

Ready to play? One person holds their can to their ear while the other speaks into theirs. The story is that if the string is tight, the sound will travel from the "speaking can" through the string and into your "listening" can like a real phone. Me? I'm not so sure it works, but it's tons of fun to play with!

Compass

Need a compass to find out which way is north?

Stroke a piece of wire against a magnet, stroking only in one direction. Scientists will tell you that this aligns the wire's atoms. (I say it's magic!) Now, thread a sewing needle and hang it above the wire. Did the needle point north when it got close to the wire? If only we had a compass to tell us if our compass is pointing north. Doh!

Build a Project

Use scrap wood hanging around the house or ask your parents to take you to the hardware store to buy a kit or the materials you need to build something specific.

Ideas: bird house, dog house, doll bed, sandbox, toy boat… what else?

Slingshot

Safety First: Slingshots can be dangerous. Make sure you watch where you aim and what types of things you hit. Don't ever aim at people or animals. (Or windows! They are expensive to replace.)

To make a slingshot, find a strong stick in the shape of a "Y." Next, you'll need a strip of stretchy rubber or elastic. It will need to be about twice as long as the space between the top of your stick's Y. Tie one end of the rubber or elastic to the top, left side of the Y, then tie the other end to the right side.

Ready? Aim! Fire! Wait! You need something to shoot out of your slingshot. How about acorns? Pebbles? Again, be careful where you aim.

It can be tricky to get a homemade slingshot to work right the first time. Be patient and make adjustments until you get it to work the way you want.

Periscope

This is so cool! My older brother made one of these in Scouts as a kid and I loved spying on customers who came to our front door to buy honey from my parents. Who will you spy on?

You will need: two empty rectangle milk cartons (half gallon (2 liters)), two small mirrors (square—as long as the milk carton is wide, if you can. If you can't find mirrors the right size, simply line your mirrors up in the center of the carton when adding them to your periscope), tape—clear packing tape is good, scissors.

Cut the tops off the two milk cartons—you might need an adult to help with this. Along the bottom of one carton, cut a hole all the way across the bottom and up about 3 inches (8 cm). You should have a rectangular hole when you're done. Do the same with the other carton.

Place one of the mirrors in the bottom of the first carton. Where do you place it? Reach inside the hole you made and tape your mirror against the back wall so it sits at a 45 degree angle. That means you will be taping it partway along the bottom of the carton as well as the back wall so it is *not* flat against the back wall. Now do the same with the other carton.

On to the final stage. Take your two cartons and where you cut the tops off, line them up to make one long carton tube. You want one carton with it's mirror hole pointing one direction and the other carton with its mirror hole pointing out in the opposite direction. You don't want both holes on the same side. Tape the two cartons together.

If you did it right, you should be able to look in one hole and see out the top of your periscope—thanks to the mirrors inside! Try it out behind the couch—pop your periscope over the top of the couch while hiding behind it and see if you can see what's on the other side of the couch! Isn't that cool? I think it's time for a spy game! (Find more spy play ideas in the "Pretend You're a Spy" game in the Let's Pretend section.)

Apple Wrinkly Faces

Safety First: Ask an adult to peel the skin off a whole apple.

Using a plastic knife, carve a face into the apple. Leave the apple in the sun for a few days so it can dry out and wrinkle. Within a few days, the face will be wrinkled and brown like a wizened old cowboy.

Potato Stamp (Sponge Stamp)
You will need: potato, knife, pen or marker, paint, and paper.

Safety First: Ask an adult to cut a potato in half—it doesn't matter which direction.

Pat the cut part of the potato dry, then draw a simple design (like a heart or a star) that can be easily cut out. This shape will be your stamp.

More Safety: Ask an adult to cut part of the potato away from the *outside* of your design so the shape sticks out from the cut side of the potato. You don't have to cut much of the potato away.

Once it is cut out, dip your stamp in paint and stamp away!

Variation: You can do this with firm sponges, too, instead of potatoes.

Bird Feeder
You will need: 2 L milk jug (plastic or cardboard), scissors, bird seed, and twine or heavy string.

Safety First: Have an adult make two square holes/windows on opposite sides of the jug using scissors or a knife. Place the holes 1 ½ inches (4 cm) up from the bottom of the jug. The square hole should be about 4 inches tall (10 cm) and 3 inches wide (7 cm). The hole needs to be big enough that birds can land on the bottom of the hole and stand there to eat the seed inside the jug.

To hang the jug, cut two small holes opposite each other 3-4 inches (7-10 cm) down from the top of the jug. Place twine through the holes and use it to tie the feeder to a tree branch.

Hint: For birds to find your feeder, you may need to leave it on the ground with seed scattered around it for a few hours to a few days until birds get used to it. Then, you can move it in stages towards and into the tree.

Bonus building activities…
- Birdhouse
- Garden Stepping Stone

Time Capsule

A time capsule is a container that is filled with things that are locked up for a few years, then opened on a special future date. Some time capsules are opened a year later, while some aren't opened for 100 years! When do you want to open your time capsule?

Let's make one! Your time capsule needs to be closeable so let's choose a container with a lid—shoeboxes and ice-cream pails make good time-capsule containers.

Now we need to put some things inside. What do you think might be interesting to find in your time capsule when you open it later? Toys? A letter to yourself (Need ideas? Check out "Letter to Yourself" and "Future Self" in the Literary Play section)? A newspaper from today? Mementos? (Don't put things in the time capsule that you will miss such as a favorite toy or will go bad such as food.)

Close your time capsule and on the lid write when you want to open it. Then put it in a safe place and try to forget about it—but also remember to open it on your assigned date. Hmm. Forget, but remember. Tricky.

HOLIDAYS

Children's experiences grow their brains.

Gabrielle Principe
Your Brain on Childhood

Although these activities are holiday themed, it doesn't mean that you can't make Christmas cards in June or can't decorate Easter eggs in November.

Make a Birthday/Christmas Wish List
What would you like? Dream big, dream small. Think creative. Want a party, but don't want all those gifts? Try these ideas…

Book Exchange
Each party guest brings one new book, wrapped. At the end of the party each party-goer is handed one present which they take home—a new book!
Variation: Place a number on each gift book and put each number in a hat as well. Draw a number and match it up with your new book!

Donate to a Charity
Each guest brings a small donation (optional) instead of a gift and the donations all go toward helping others in need. Charities can include pet shelters, natural disasters, building a water well in a developing country, cancer research… the list is endless. What cause is important to you, your family, and your child?

Musical Pass the Present
Wrap a small gift in a box and add several layers of wrapping paper. All players sit in a circle and someone turns on the music. When the music stops, the person holding the gift unwraps the first layer of wrapping paper. The music starts up again and everyone passes the gift again. When the music stops again, the person holding the gift unwraps the next layer of paper… and on you go until there is no more paper. The person who unwraps the last layer gets to keep the gift.

Pin the Tail on the Donkey
No need to stop at pinning the tail on the donkey. Pin the beard on Santa. The candles on the birthday cake… And no need to use pins. Simply use tape!

Don't know how to play? Grab a picture of a donkey, Santa, or whatever you happen to have on hand that is about a foot and a half by a foot in a half in terms of size. (Or bigger!) You will need something to pin—a tail, beard, nose, hat, candle—made out of paper or cardboard. You can have one that all the players use or one for each player.

Blindfold the player who is pinning and spin them several times so they don't know where the picture is, then guide them in the direction. They have to blindly pin the item on the picture, trying to get it as close to its proper spot as possible. The one who is closest, wins.

Make sure you label whose tail is whose. Or if sharing one tail to reuse, simply use a small sticker with the players initials on it and place the sticker where their tail landed.

Search for a Groundhog
Did the groundhog see its shadow this year? See if you can find him—maybe you can see his shadow—or not.

Make Valentine's Day Cards
Using the potato stamp craft (found in the Construction Crafts section), you can make easy, fun, heart stamp cards for the whole class.

Paper Hearts

Decorate Easter Eggs
Want easy? Me, too!

Take a few hardboiled eggs and soak them in water colored with food coloring until they've soaked up the color. Bam! That's easy!

Tip: Stickers and markers can also make your eggs look great.

Hint: You can also buy special kits that are a bit more involved in arts and crafts stores.

Bunny Ears
Want a printable template you can cut out? You can find my template online at: http://itsallkidsplay.ca/wp-content/uploads/2012/04/Bunny_Ears.pdf

Look for a Leprechaun
Where do you think they hide with their pots of gold? Think you can catch one?

Carve a Jack-O-Lantern
Safety First: If you're too small to use a knife for carving, draw your design with marker on your pumpkin and have an adult cut out.

Hint: Some craft stores have kid-friendly carving tools that are safer than a kitchen knife.

Toast Pumpkin Seeds

You will need: pumpkin seeds, 1 ½ tbsp salt (23 mL) for every ¾ cup (180 mL) of seeds, a strainer, baking sheet, oven, oven mitts, and help from an adult.

Scoop the seeds out of a pumpkin and place them in a strainer, separating them from any of the pumpkin's stringy goo. Rinse the seeds under warm water, then shake the strainer so the seeds aren't drippy. Lay the seeds on a cookie sheet and sprinkle with salt.

Safety First: Have an adult place them in an oven at 300F (175 C) for 20-30 minutes until the seeds are dry and crisp.

Let them cool and enjoy!

Tissue Ghosts

This is a super easy Halloween craft that only takes a few minutes and is great for all ages.

You will need: 2 facial tissues, string, and a black marker.

Lay one facial tissue out flat. Scrunch the other tissue into a ball and lay it in the middle of the flat tissue. Gather the four corners of the flat tissue, keeping the scrunched tissue in the middle. Tie a piece of string under the head to keep the tissue from falling out—this is the ghost's head and you don't want it falling off. Bonk!

Use a marker to draw a face on your ghost. And… you're done!

Prepare a Gift for a Needy Child or Family

Get some friends together and put a few small gifts and food together for a needy family. You can do this locally or send it to a child or family in another country. Some organizations need donations all year, while some help out during emergencies or special times of the year.

Candy Christmas Tree

An edible craft—the best kind!

You will need: a pointy ended ice cream cone, green icing, and candies.

Cover the ice cream cone with icing and stick your candies on the tree and voila! You have a yummy tree. Kids looooove making this craft—and eating it, too.

Write to Santa Claus

In Canada if you write a letter to Santa Claus during November and early December, he will write back. Don't forget to give him your return mailing address.

Santa's Canadian address:
Santa Claus
The North Pole, Canada
HOH OHO

Santa's American (United States) address:
North Pole Christmas Cancellation Postmaster 5400 Mail Trail Fairbanks AK 99709-9998

A few more ideas...
- Decorate for the Holidays
- Gingerbread House
- Make Christmas Cards
- Sing Christmas Carols
- Make Christmas Tree Ornaments
- New Year's Resolution

PLAY WITH A FRIEND

> When people play, they become attuned to each other.
>
> Stuart Brown
Play

You will need more than one person for the activities in this chapter, so grab a friend! Did you know that playing with a friend can help develop communication skills, problem solving skills, social competency, critical thinking, conflict resolution skills (including dealing with disappointment, cooperation, and compromise), as well as emotional intelligence? Plus, it's a lot of fun! And according to David Elkind (author of *The Power of Play*), it helps develop fairness, justice, trust, empathy, caring, and sharing.

Penny Rugby (Quarters)
You will need a friend, a table, and a penny (or other coin).

Each person sits across from each other at a small table. One person goes first (player 1). Player 1 starts with the penny overhanging (balanced half on and half off the table) their end of the table. Player 1 flicks the penny with their fingers or bumps it with their hand up to 3 times to move it across the table—they are trying to get the coin to overhang the edge of the other side of the table by the end of their turn. If the penny goes off the table or doesn't overhang on the other end, they don't get points and the turn goes to the other player (player 2). If it overhangs, player 1 gets 5 points and a chance to go to goal.

To go to goal, player 1 spins the penny on the table and catches it between their thumbs while it's still spinning. (If they don't catch it between their thumbs, their turn ends). If they catch it, player 2 makes a goalpost by placing their thumbs together and spreading their hands out, elbows on the table. Player 1 keeps holding the penny between their thumbs, then "throws" the penny through the goal (2 more points if they get it between the posts). Whether it goes in or not, it is now player 2's turn.

Keep playing until you get bored or a player reaches the number of points the players have decided will end the game. (Say, 15 points.)

Hot-Cold
One player hides an item or toy (they are the hider) and the other player tries to find it (they are the seeker).

As the seeker looks for the item, the hider says, "You're getting hotter" if the seeker is getting closer to the hidden item. Or they say, "You're getting colder" if the seeker is getting farther from the hidden object.

Staring Contest
Channel your inner fish (they don't blink). Two people stare at each other. The first person to blink loses.

Copycat
Copy everything someone else does. Anything they say, you say. Anything they do, you do. This is a MOST excellent way to annoy your brother or sister. Especially when they say, "Stop that!" and you then say "Stop that!" in the exact same way. Have fun!

Liar's Club
You won't really be a liar, you will tell what's called "tall tales."

Get some friends together and see who can make up the biggest, silliest story that is not true. For example, my aunt once made up a story where my dad took a huge jump on his windsurfer and ended up landing in the back of a semi-truck!

Reverse Roles
You pretend to be your friend. They pretend to be you. What do they say? How do they act? How do they dress? How do they walk? What do they think about French toast or world peace?

Mirror
Once person moves and makes faces while the other person stands in front of them and pretends they are a mirror. The mirror tries to do the exact same things at the same time as the other person.

Play...
- Chinese Checkers
- Checkers
- Chess
- Patty Cake
- Peek-A-Boo
- Pillow Fight
- Old Maid (Card Game)
- Bingo
- Cat's Cradle
- Tic-Tac-Toe (Xs & Os)
- Marbles
- Tennis
- Racquetball
- Frisbee
- Arm Wrestle

Board Game
If you are tired of your board games, ask your parents if you can trade with a friend, or change the rules to an existing game.

Cops and Robbers
A childhood classic!

Who are the police officers and who are the robbers? Robbers try to get away while the police officers try to catch them and put them in jail!

Coin Relay
This is a great birthday party game and definitely a challenge. (Younger kids may find this game too challenging.)

Place a few coins in a shallow dish and give each player a plastic fork. (You will need several coins, two flat dishes and one plastic fork per player.) With the fork's handle in their mouth the player tries to scoop coins onto the fork's tines. They then carry the fork—still in their mouth (no hands!) over to another dish without dropping the coins off their fork.

At the end of the game, the player with the most coins in their new dish wins. Any dropped coins don't count.

Spoon Water Races
This game is best played outside as it can get a bit wet. You will need a couple of friends, water, containers and spoons.

The idea is to empty one small container of water into another. The trick is, you can only use a spoon to take the water from one container to the other. The further the containers are apart, the harder it will be. See who can get the most in the empty container the fastest.

Ring-Around-The-Rosie
Toddlers and preschoolers love this one. Hold hands, forming a circle, facing in. As you go around in the circle, sing:

Ring around the rosie, a pocket full of posies. Husha-husha we all fall down.
Then everyone falls down. Want another versus? While still on the ground, sing:

Cows are in the meadow, eating buttercups. Husha-husha we all stand up.
Everyone stands up again.

London Bridge is Falling Down

Another toddler and preschooler favorite. Two adults stand with their hands together to make a bridge for the kids to go under as you sing the song. As you get to 'lady-o' you snag the child who is now zipping under the bridge (or maybe waiting, hoping to get caught!). Lyrics:

London bridge is falling down, falling down, falling down. London bridge is falling down, my fair lady-o.

Play Salon

Do each other's hair and fingernails. (Ask your parents before you bring out the nail polish! Or makeup.)

What Am I Drawing?

Using your finger for a pencil, gently draw on a friend's back. They will then try to guess what you're drawing or writing on their back.

Hangman

You will need: paper, pen or pencil, and two players.

One player thinks of a word or a short phrase and draws a dash (a short line) on a piece of paper for each letter in the word or phrase. The other player tries to guess the word/phrase letter by letter. For each letter guessed correctly, the letter gets written on top of its dash. Each time a letter gets guessed incorrectly, a body part is drawn onto a hangman. The player keeps guessing letters until they can guess the word/phrase or the hangman gets "hanged." He gets hung when there are no more parts to draw. If the player guesses the word/phrase before the hangman is hung, they win.

Hangman body parts: head, body, leg, leg, arm, arm, face.

Hint: Write out the alphabet and cross off each letter as it is guessed to help keep track of which letters have been guessed already.

Name that Tune

Take turns humming songs you know. One player hums, the others guess. No words or actions are allowed. (Unless you decide they are allowed as hints.)

Make a New Friend

Who is that new kid on the block? That person making a sandcastle over there? Go introduce yourself!

Memory

Take a deck of playing cards and arrange them face down on a table or the floor.

The first player flips over two cards, leaving them in their spot as they flip them over. If they are a pair, the player takes them and flips over two more cards. They keep flipping two cards at a time until they don't flip over pairs at the same time. If they flip over two cards that are not a pair, they turn them face down again and that's the end of their turn.

The player who makes the most number of pairs wins the game.

Tip: This game can also be played alone.

Variation: You can play with the whole deck (52 cards) and make it so you have to match not only the same number, but colors, too. Or you can choose to play with only half the deck to make it easier.

Steam Roller

Lie on the floor and roll over each other.

Warning: Watch out for bigger people—they might squish you!

People Pile/Dog Pile

Get a bunch of people together and pile on top of each other!

People Sandwich

Pile three people on top of each other as shown on the book's cover. The bottom person is the bread, the middle person can be sandwich meat, lettuce or tomato and the top person is another slice of bread.

Hint: If you have a really small person they can go on the very top as a pickle.

Horse Rides

Get down on all fours and let someone small climb on your back. Crawl around with them on your back and neigh like a horse! What other animals can you be?

Piggyback Rides

Airplane Rides

Lie on your back. Have someone smaller than you stand by your feet. Place your feet on their stomach and hold their hands tightly. Carefully pull your legs up until they are sticking straight up and the person is laying on your feet above you, facing you. They are now an airplane flying through the sky!

Thumb War

One, two, three, four, I declare a thumb war! Thumbs, get in your corners. Ready? Three, two, one, go!

Two players face each other. The players hold right hands, curling their fingers into each other's palms so their hands "lock." Both players touch the tips of their thumbs together. Ready? Go! See which player can pin down the other player's thumb under their thumb for three seconds.

Three Way Thumb War

Can you do three hands in one war? Three players all hold their hands out flat, thumbs up. Then you all curl your hands into one fist together. It sounds crazy, but it actually works! My daughter and her cousins discovered this while out camping. You'll have to try it to believe it!

Truth, Dare, Double Dare, Promise to Repeat

With several friends, go around in a circle taking turns. One player chooses truth, dare, double dare, or promise to repeat. Then one of the other players chooses what that person will do/say during their turn. To keep the game fun, keep it lighthearted and silly.

Truth: The player asks them a question they have to answer truthfully. Example: Do you have a crush on Bob from gym class?
Dare: Dare them to do something zany. Example: Dare them to ask your sibling to marry them.
Double Dare: The extra big dare. Example: Double dare them to ask your sibling to marry them as well as place a kiss on their cheek.
Promise to Repeat: They promise to repeat something you say.

Theme Party
Have friends over for a sleepover or an afternoon of fun.

Pick your theme (superheroes, princesses, camping, spies, jungle animals). If it is a camping party, ask your guests to bring things like sleeping bags and flashlights. You can camp out in the backyard and do camping activities like sing campfire songs, make s'mores, cook hot dogs, etc.

Prisoner Lift
With a friend, sit on the floor back to back. Now, link your arms together at the elbow. Can you stand up together with your elbows linked together?

BUMP/HORSE
You will need two players, a basketball, and a basketball net.

Each player takes turns tossing the ball in the net. If a player misses, they get a letter in the word "bump" (or "horse"). The player that spells "bump" first, is bumped out of the game.

Variations:
Anywhere: Players can shoot from anywhere.
Catch and Shoot: Players can only shoot from where they caught the ball.
Key: The first player shoots from the top of the key. If they get the ball in the net, they can keep shooting until they miss. When they miss the next player shoots from where they caught the ball. If it goes in, they go to the top of the key and shoot until they miss. When they miss, the next player shoots from where they caught the ball.
Challenges: Players can make challenges. To make a challenge, one player makes a hard or tricky shot. The next player then has to make the same shot. If they get the ball in the net, they decide how the next shot will be made. If a player misses a challenge, they get a letter, plus they have to keep trying to make the other player's shots until they make one. Then they can issue their own challenge.

Ice-Cube Curling
On a smooth surface, mark a circle. Then take ice-cubes and try to slide them across the surface and get them to stop in the circle. Can you do it? Better make sure you play this one somewhere that can get wet as the ice cubes melt!

Ninja
Two players. (You can also play in a big group.)

Players stand facing each other and within reach. Without moving their feet, players try to move like ninjas (it's actually more like a robot) and chop the other player's arm before they move it out of the way. Players can only move their arms at the shoulder and elbow—sort of like robots. They can also bend at the waist. But they can't move their feet!

One player moves their arm, trying to chop the other player while they anticipate the move and try to move out of the way. One move only! You can't do three moves to try and get away from one chop. So as the ninja comes in for the chop by dropping their arm, you must drop your arm first! If you get chopped, that arm goes behind your back. Out of arms? You're out of the game.

21/Blackjack
This game can be played alone or with others and is a fun way to improve math skills. You will need a deck of playing cards. Just… um, no gambling, okay?

Players try to get their cards to add up to 21 or as close to it without going over. (If a player goes over 21 they are out.) Whoever is the closest to 21, wins.

Aces can count as 1 or as 11, whichever is better for your hand. Jacks, queens, and kings are all worth 10. The number cards are worth their number. (So a 5 is worth 5.)

All players get dealt two cards. One card is dealt face up, the other one, face down. The players look at their face down card without showing the other players. They add up their two cards in their head and   decide if they want another card to try and get closer to 21 or not. If they want another card they say, "hit me," if they don't want another card as they are afraid they'll go over 21, they say, "stay."

Tip: If your cards add up to 10 or less, always ask for another card as you cannot go over 21 from 10.

When everyone has decided to "stay" and not be dealt more cards, they add up their hand and whomever is closer to 21 wins. If a player has 21, they automatically win. More than one player can get 21, but the player with fewer cards wins.

War
You will need 2 decks of playing cards and another player.

Each player gets a deck of cards (make sure you shuffle them well). Players face each other. At the same time, each player takes the top card off their deck and places it face up. Whichever player has the highest card wins the other person's card. (Aces are the highest card, kings are second highest (13), then queen (12), jack (11).) For example: Jo has a 6 and Sally has a king. Sally's king (13) wins Jo's 6.

If both players deal the same card, there is a tie and players go to war. Each player then deals four cards, face down and off to the side. Then at the same time, players show the top card off their deck. The highest card wins the war. That means they win all the cards from that round (the first deal which was tied, both stacks of four face down cards, plus the last two cards that were dealt).

If this war happens to be a tie as well, then deal four more cards face down plus one face up. Whoever has the highest face up card, wins.

When players reach the end of their deck, they flip over their "dealt" stack and use the cards they have won as their new deck. When one player runs out of cards completely, the game is over. This can take a realllllllllly long time sometimes! (Unless your brother cheats. Not pointing any fingers. Nope. Okay, I am.)

Shiverees
Ready to get shiveree?

On a friend's back, slowly and gently draw a big "X" with your finger. While doing that say: "Criss Cross."
Then slide a hand slowly and gently down their back. Say: "Applesauce."
Walk your fingers up their back, one by one. Say: "Spiders crawling up your back."
Tickle their left side, then their right side. Say: "One here, one there."
Run your fingers around on their scalp (head). Say: "Spiders crawling through your hair."
Give them a little squeeze. Say: "Tight squeeze."
Blow gently on their neck. Say: "Cool breeze. Now you've got the shiverees!"

Did they get goosebumps all the way from their toes to their nose? I did just writing out the instructions!

Draw a Picture Together
With a friend, draw a picture together. Use one piece of paper and work together to make one drawing.

Three Player People
Three players draw one person—but without seeing what the other players have already drawn!

Fold a piece of paper into three. The first player draws a head above the first fold without showing anyone else what they have drawn. (They make sure the neck lines come just below the first fold. When they draw the head.) They then fold over the paper so nobody can see the head they drew.

The next player adds a body onto the neck and folds the paper so the next player can't see the body. The last player adds legs, still not knowing what sort of person the other two players drew.

Unfold for the big reveal! Does the person everyone drew look funny or is it actually pretty good?

Slapees
You and a friend face each other. You hold your hands out flat, palms down, so your fingertips almost touch each other. Name of the game? Slapees! Try to slap the other person's hand before they can pull it away. Anyone can try to slap the other player's hand at any time!

Treasure Map Hide-and-Seek
My kids love this one and it's great for teaching map skills and developing spatial awareness.

You will need: Two players, paper, pencils, a teddy bear (or other object) to hide.

Hide the teddy bear somewhere in the house. Draw a map of your house, or the room the teddy bear is hidden in and draw an "X" where you hid it. Now, hand the map to the other player(s) and see if they can use the map to find the hidden bear.

Treasure Hunt

Set one up for your friends, or have someone set one up for you. You will need a map to the treasure, maybe some clues and of course, some treasures!

Pick a Hand

With your hands behind your back, place a small item in your right or left hand. Then have your friend try and guess which hand is hiding the object. No cheating!

Scavenger Hunt

This game can be played alone, together with a friend or with teams.

Search for the items on the list below or make your own list:
toothpick
rock the size of your pinky fingernail
ring
feather
penny
dust bunny
pillow
something you would read
something with the letter 'J' on it
salt
insect
leaf
glue
monkey (not a real one!)

Hide-it, Find-it, Repeat

This is a game my brother and mom had going on for YEARS. They used a plastic flower, but you can use any object that works for you. First my brother hid the flower in my mom's work lunch kit. When she found it, she hid it where my brother would find it. When he found it, he hid it again for Mom. Eventually the hiding spots got harder and harder... I'm not sure they ever found the last hiding spot...

This is a great game for learning patience! It's so difficult waiting for the other person to find the object sometimes!

Wheel Barrow Races
Put someone in a wheel barrow and go!

Human Wheel Barrow Races
Number of players: 4 or more to race.

2 people become wheel barrows and the other 2 become the pushers.

The wheel barrows lie on their stomachs and push their chests off the ground. The pushers lift the wheel barrow's legs by holding their ankles. The wheel barrows should now be off the ground with their hands holding them up. To move, the wheel barrows walk ahead on their hands. Take it slow at first and before you know it you will be racing!

Categories
Everyone sits in a circle and claps or slaps their legs to a rhythm (like clap-clap, clap, clap-clap, clap or slap-slap, slap, slap-slap, slap). One player starts the categories by saying "I am thinking of kinds of…." They say this in rhythm to the clapping or slapping. The next player in the circle joins in after one clap or slap by saying something that fits in the category.

Go around the circle until all players are out of ideas or someone misses a beat. Players can be sent out of the game for missing a beat, or they can keep playing.

Example:
Person one: (clap) "I am thinking of kinds of clothes" (clap) "hat" (clap)
Person two: "socks" (clap)
Person three: "pants" (clap)
Persons four: "t-shirt" (clap)

Category ideas: clothes, candy, places, things that grow, TV shows, books, people, relatives, food that is red, animals, electronics, teachers in your school, sports, dog breeds, song titles, names, school subjects.

What Do You Remember?
Place several small items on a small tray or plate and let everyone have a chance to memorize the items. Only unlike the game above, take the *whole* tray away and players try to remember what items were on the tray. The person who has written down the most number of correct items wins.

Memory Take-Away

Place several small items on a small tray or plate and let everyone have a chance to memorize the items. One player takes an item away, hiding it behind their back while the other players cover their eyes. They then uncover their eyes, look at the tray, and try to guess which item was taken away.

Preschoolers can be surprisingly good at this game.

What Am I?

All players get a photo or name of something taped to their back. They ask others "yes" or "no" questions to try and guess who or what they are. For example, "Am I a superhero?" Yes. "Do I wear red?" No.

Bonus fun...
- Tickle Fest with Friends
- Have a Race
- Have a Sleepover
- Pull Someone in a Wagon
- Pull Someone on a Blanket
- Start Your Own Club
- Join or Make a Parade
- Tell Jokes
- Trade Stickers or other Collectibles with a Friend
- Teach a Friend to do Something You Can Do

ACTIVE GROUP GAMES

Movement play strengthens the brain and fosters learning, innovation, flexibility, adaptability, and resilience.

Stuart Brown
Play

In our brains, perception and action are linked. We use our bodies to learn about the world… We do things to the world with our bodies to see what happens, and our brain crunches the numbers and draws conclusions.

Gabrielle Principe
Your Brain on Childhood

Are you ready to get active? These games are for larger groups of kids—great for birthday parties, the classroom (recess or gym class), summer camp, large family gatherings, or anywhere you find large groups of kids (or adults!) who are ready to play.

Are you ready to rumble? There's a lot of talk these days about rough play. Kids are curbed at recess from getting too rough as we worry about hurting others. And there is some legitimate concern there, however, we also have to remember that some rough-and-tumble play is needed to help develop and maintain social awareness, cooperation, empathy, and altruism. Rough play, according to Stuart Brown (author of *Play: How it Shapes the Brain, Opens the Imagination, and Invigorates the Soul*) is actually friendship play. When rough-and-tumble play is cut out of childhood, it is found to lead to poor control of violent impulses later in life. In other words, *some* rough and tumble play is natural.

Red Light, Green Light
Number of players: 4 or more. A preschooler favorite!

One player is the light. They stand away from the group with their back facing the group. When the light says, "green light," everyone moves toward the light. When the light says, "red light," everyone must freeze as the light quickly turns around. If anyone is still moving, the light calls them by name and sends them back to the starting point. When a player makes it to where the light is standing without being caught, they are the light for the next game.

British Bulldog
Number of players: 10 or more.

3 players hold hands and stand in a line in the middle of the playing area. These players are bulldogs. When they are ready, they yell "British Bulldog" and the other players try to run to the other end of the field without being touched by the bulldogs. When they are touched by the bulldogs, they join them for the next round. Keep going until everyone has become a bulldog.

Netball/Human Foosball

You will need a soccer ball and net (or pylons or something to shoot between). 14 players.

This game is like soccer and foosball all rolled into one.

Divide the playing area into three zones (two end zones and one middle zone) that go across the playing area with nets at the end. Each team has seven players—one in net and two in each zone. Players must stay in their zone or the net like they are 'attached' to their spot as though they were human foosball players.

Players can't run and kick the ball around the field (no dribbling). They can only receive and pass the ball and they can't move out of their zone. (No hands, either! Unless in net.) When passing, a player has three seconds to pass and they can't skip a zone. So, if they are in the first zone, they have to pass to the middle zone, they can't shoot all the way down the other end zone.

Dodge Ball

Number of players: 8-16 people. You will need: a large open space and 3 balls.

Divide the playing field into two sides. Players from one side cannot cross over to the other team's side.

Each team tries to win by getting everyone on the other team out. If a player gets hit with a ball thrown by the other team, they are out. If they catch a ball thrown by the other team, the person who threw the ball is out. Players who try to catch a ball, but drop it are out. If the ball hits more than one player before hitting the ground, all the hit players are out. Players have 5 seconds to throw the ball after picking it up or catching it or they are out. When all players on one team are out the other team wins. If you hit someone in the head with a ball, you are out for the rest of the game and cannot be brought back in, even if someone catches the other team's throw.

To get a player back in the game that was out, someone on their team must catch a ball thrown by the other team. So if a thrown ball is caught, the person who threw it is out and someone on the team who caught the ball gets to come back into the game.

A ball can be killed (can't get anyone out) if it is bumped with another ball that is being held by a player.

Shark Tank/Shark and Fishes
Create a shark tank zone—it can be marked by pylons or players can simply remember the area they need to stay in.

Several players are sharks who try and catch the fishes that come into their tank for soccer balls or other items. The fishes try to run into the shark tank to try and retrieve items without being eaten! Run, run, run!

Trust Falls
This game is best for ages 12 and up.

Number of players: 9 players and an adult to help make sure the trust falls stay safe.

One person stands on a solid platform (no higher than waist high) with their back facing the group. The platform should make their feet almost as high as the hands that they will be falling onto.

Everyone else stands facing each other in 2 lines (4 players in each line). The two lines place their arms out, palms up with their elbows bent as though they are holding a tray. The two lines need to stand close enough that everyone's hands and arms alternate and mix with each other and create one long line. Try to make the line of arms flat. Place pillows and extra padding underneath the line of arms—just in case.

When the line is ready, the person on the platform crosses their arms over their chest and makes themselves straight as a board—**this is very important!** If they bend, they will fall through the arms! When they are ready, they will fall backwards into the waiting hands.

Tug-o-War
Number of players: 2 or more. You will need: a line (even if it is just a towel) and a long rope.

Divide into two teams. One team stands on one side of the line, holding onto their end of the rope. On the other side of the line, the other team holds onto the other end of the rope.

PULL! Whichever teams pulls the other team over the line, wins. Can all of the kids at a party beat the adults? Try!

Knock Your Socks Off

Divide the group of players (6-16 players works well) into two teams. Everyone needs to be wearing socks.

The teams get down on their hands and knees as this is a crawling game—you cannot stand up or stand on your feet at *any* point during the game. Choose an area for the game such as the living room. (If you leave the boundaries of the game area, you are automatically out.)

When the game starts, the two teams begin crawling around, trying to pull the socks off the other team's feet. The goal is to get all the socks off the other team. Once a sock is off a foot, it stays off. Once a player has no socks left on, they move to the sidelines to cheer on the other players (they are out of the game).

No kicking! And no grabbing at your own sock if someone is pulling it off. And no knee-high socks or stirrup pants (remember those?)—they are so unfair (according to the other team. Whoops. Sorry!)

What Time is it Mr. Wolf?

Number of players: 4 or more.

One player is the wolf and everyone else stands far away at a starting point. The wolf keeps their back to the other players (and cannot peek). Everyone asks together, "What time is it Mr. Wolf?" The wolf says a time. If he says "12 o'clock," everyone takes 12 steps towards the wolf. After everyone has moved forward, they ask the time again. If the wolf replies, "Time to eat you!" then everyone runs back to the starting point. The wolf tries to tag players as they run back. If a player is caught before they get back to the starting point (where they will be safe), they are out.

Keep playing until all players are caught. The last player caught by the wolf, becomes the wolf for the next game.

Variation: Eaten players join the wolf so there become more and more wolves as the game goes on.

Red Rover
Number of players: 8 or more.

Divide the players into 2 teams. The teams each form a line and hold hands facing each other. One team calls out "Red rover, red rover, we call _____ (name of a player from the other team) over." And they call over someone from the other team. That player runs over and tries to break the line by running between two players, making them let go. If they break the line, they take a player from the other team back to join their team. If they don't break through, they join the other team.

Safety First: Be gentle and keep held hands low so the player who was called over doesn't get hit above the chest. If someone's going to get hurt—let go! It's no fun if other players get hurt. Winning is not everything.

Pig in the Middle
You will need: three people and a ball.

Two players throw or roll a ball between themselves. The third player is the pig. The pig stays between the other two players and tries to get the ball. When the pig gets the ball, the player who threw or rolled the caught ball becomes the pig.

Variation: Instead of a ball, use a Frisbee.

Three-Legged Races
Number of players: 4 to race. You will need: old nylons or scarves to tie legs together.

Stand beside your partner and tie one of your legs to one of theirs. (For example, your left leg and their right leg or your right leg and their left leg.) Now try walking and running!

Ultimate/Ultimate Frisbee
Number of players: 10-20

Ultimate is just like football, but played with a Frisbee. Well, except you can't run with the Frisbee. You can take three steps, but then have to toss it to another player.

Capture the Flag
Number of players: 10 or more.

You will need: two flags (or towels) and lots of space to play.

Divide the players into two teams. Divide the playing area into two sides with a line between the two sides. If you are playing in the yard, one side could be the front yard and the other team's side could be the backyard.

Each team takes a few minutes to hide their flag on their playing side and decide where their jail will be (it can be a tree, wagon, or blanket…). Once both teams have hidden their flag, the two sides try to capture the other side's flag without being caught by someone on the other team.

If a player is off their team's playing side, they can get caught by the other team and taken to the other team's jail. Only a member of your own team can free you from jail by tagging you—as long as they don't get caught, too! If all of one team gets put in the other team's jail at once, the other team wins, even if they haven't captured the flag.

If a player with the other team's flag gets caught before getting back to their side where they'll be safe, the flag is taken from them and put back in its hiding spot. If one team gets the other team's flag back to their side, they win.

Man Tracker
Can you track and find your friends? Divide the group into trackers and hiders. One group goes out in a predetermined area (create boundaries!) and hides. The trackers then try to find them using clues such as knocked down grass, footprints in the dirt, or giggling hiders.

Let's play...
- Basketball
- Badminton
- Soccer
- Football
- Sack Races
- Crack the Whip
- Baseball/Softball
- Lawn Darts
- Darts
- Ping Pong
- Pick-up-Sticks
- Jacks

TAG & HIDE AND SEEK

But learning is not only in the head. It is also in the hands and feet and arms and legs. The entire body from head to toe is one big instrument of learning.

Gabrielle Principe
Your Brain on Childhood

Tag

Number of players: Best with 4 or more.

One player is "it." The "it" player tries to tag (lightly touch) one of the other players making them "it." Once another player becomes "it" the used-to-be "it" player has to get away from the "it" player just like everyone else or they will be tagged and become "it" again.

Variation: Can't Tag Your Butcher: You need at least 5 people to play this version. Once a player becomes "it" they can't tag the player who made them "it" (their butcher).

Freeze Tag

When a player is tagged, they become frozen (can't move). Frozen players stand with their arms spread out until someone who isn't frozen can run under their arms to unfreeze them. Play until everyone is frozen or until the "it" player becomes too tired and needs to swap out.

Blob Tag

When the "it" player tags another player, they also become "it." "It" players hold hands to make a blob and try to make all the players part of their blob. The last player tagged is the new "it" player for the next game.

Shadow Tag

"It" tags the shadows of other players by stepping on them instead of touching players. (This version of tag can lead to quite a few "you didn't tag me!" arguments since players can't feel it. Consider yourself warned.)

Flashlight Tag

It must be dark for this one. Agree on where the game boundaries are (fenced yard or basement). Each player gets a flashlight but only the person who is "it" turns theirs on. Everyone runs around and every few seconds "it" turns on their flashlight for one second to try and tag a player by shining the light on them during their second. Once tagged, that player can help with tagging other players in the same way.

Zombie Tag

The "it" player turns others into zombies when they tag them. The players who have been tagged then walk around moaning while holding their arms out front like a zombie. The "it" player tries to turn everyone into zombies and once they do, the game is over.

Infection Tag

This game makes everyone "it" quickly! (This one is like blog tag, only "it" players don't stick together as a blob.)

One player starts as "it." As they tag other players, they become "it" too until there is only one person left who isn't "it." They become "it" for the next game.

Melt Tag

Like regular tag only when players are tagged by the "it" player, they slowly melt down to the ground. If another player gets to them and tags them before they melt all the way to the ground, they are saved and can keep playing. If they melt all the way to the ground before being saved, they are either out, or out for 15 seconds—depends which way you want to play.

TV Tag

If you think you are about to be tagged by the "it" player you can save yourself in this version of tag. When about to get tagged, sit on the ground and quickly say the name of a TV show. If you can sit and say the name before you're tagged, you're safe. If not, look at who's "it" now! (You!)

Players can only say a TV show name once in a game. Once it has been said by *anyone*, nobody can use it any longer to save them—it's used up.

Tornado Tag

The "it" player spins when tagging others as though they are a tornado.

This is a good version to play if some players are bigger and older and faster—they can be tornados and the younger players can be regular players. So if an older child is "it" they have to be a tornado and spin while they are "it," but the younger players don't.

Electric Tag

When a player is tagged, they sit. They don't become "it," but if a player runs by close enough, they can tag them as though they were "it" and the tagged player then sits and tries to zap other players as they run by.

Grounders

See the Playground Fun section for the rules on this playground version of tag.

Battle Tag

You need two "it" players for this version of tag. One is a furnace and one is a freezer. They can't tag each other, but they can tag all other players as they try to take over the game by making everyone either hot or frozen.

One "it" player—the freezer—tries to make everyone "frozen." The other "it" player—the furnace—tries to make everyone "hot." Players keep running around after they're tagged, and simply state their status when an "it" player comes close. If they have been tagged by the furnace, they say "hot." If they have been tagged by the freezer, they say "frozen." If they haven't been tagged yet they say "just right." If they are "hot" and a freezer tags them, they then become "frozen."

Inverted Tag

Everyone but one player is "it." They all chase the "it" player in hopes that they will be tagged to make them "it" as well. Because being "it" is actually "not it." Wait... I'm confused!

Sponge Tag

Take your water fights and tag game to an all new hot-weather level of fun!

The "it" player has several sponges soaked with water. To tag other players, they have to hit them with a wet sponge! You might want a lot of sponges as I see this version turning into a free-for-all water fight!

Hide-and-Seek

Number of players: 2 or more.

While one player covers their eyes and counts to 20, the rest of the players hide. When the counting player reaches 20, they call out, "Ready or not, here I come!" and go search for the hidden players. In the classic game, players have to stay in their original hiding spot.

Variation: Players can switch hiding places throughout the game. That means after they know the seeker has already looked in a certain hiding spot, they can sneak over and hide in it, making it more difficult to be found. (My brother used to do this to me all the time—without telling me—and it drove me nuts! So, maybe establish this rule before you start playing.)

Sardines
Number of players: 4 or more.

Sardines is like hide-and-seek (seen above), but only 1 player hides while the rest of the players count to 20. When a player finds the hiding player, they secretly join them in the hiding spot until everyone has found the hiding spot. It can get squishy!

Kick the Can
Number of players: 4 or more. Think hide-and-seek combined with tag.

There are several variations of this game, but here are the basics:

Place a can in the middle of the playing area, like the backyard. Select one player to be "it." They are guarding the can. They cover their eyes and count to 20 and everyone else goes and hides. When the "it" player is done counting, they try to find everyone like in regular hide-and-seek. When they find someone, that player has to run and kick the can before the "it" player can tag them.

If they get to the can and kick it before getting tagged, they're safe. If they get tagged, they are the new "it" player and this round of Kick the Can ends. When the round ends because someone was tagged, the "it" player yells, "Ollie, Ollie Oxen Free." This means that it is safe for the hiding players to come out as a new game will be starting.

Hide and Seek Tag
Two great games combined into one! This one is like Kick the Can, but with a slight twist.

The "it" player covers their eyes at the "base" (can be a box, picnic table, tree, can… whatever you have). They count to 20 while the other players all hide. When the "it" player goes looking for the others, the hiders try to sneak back to the base without getting tagged. If they get tagged, they also become "it" and help look for other players to tag.

Quieter Group Games

QUIETER GROUP GAMES

Player lowers the level of violence in a society and increases communication.
Stuart Brown
Play

While these group games are less active than the ones in the previous section, they may not be, um, quieter. Have fun! (I have some earplugs you can borrow if you need them.)

Button, Button, Who Has the Button?
Number of players: 5 or more. You will need: a button (or other small object like a nickel or a marble).

Everyone sits in a circle except the guesser. The guesser sits in the middle. The players in the circle pass the button to each other behind their backs. The guesser tries to guess who has the button. If they guess right, then the player who had the button becomes the guesser. To make it trickier for the guesser, the players in the circle move their hands like they are passing the button even when they aren't.

Hot Potato
Number of players: 4 or more.

One player is a leader who stands with their back to the group. The other players stand close together and pass a potato. (The potato can be a ball or teddy bear—it doesn't have to be a real potato.) When the leader says, "potato," the player holding the potato is out. Keep playing until one player is left. If the potato is in the air when the leader says "potato," nobody is out.

Simon Says
Number of players: 4 or more.

One player is "Simon." The other players stand in front of Simon and face him/her. Simon tells the group to do different actions while saying "Simon says…"

The group follows Simon's command (such as: Simone says touch your head). If they do not do it, they are out of the game.

Simon can give commands *without* saying "Simon says" as part of the command. He's trying to trick you! Listen carefully! If players do the command where Simon didn't say "Simon says," they're out of the game.

The last player still in the game becomes Simon for the next game.

Two Truths and a Lie
Tell two truths about yourself and one thing that isn't true. See if your friends can guess which one is the lie.

Farmer in the Dell
Number of players: 10 or more.

Players hold hands and dance in circle around one player who is the farmer. As everyone sings the song (below) the farmer picks someone from the circle to be his wife. The wife then picks a child, the child picks a nurse, the nurse picks a dog, the dog picks a cat, the cat picks a mouse, and finally, the mouse picks the cheese. The player who is the cheese becomes the farmer in the next round. (If you have a large group, not everyone will be chosen.)

Sing this song as everyone dances:
The farmer in the dell
The farmer in the dell
Hi-ho, the Derry-O
The farmer in the dell

The farmer takes a wife
The farmer takes a wife
Hi-Ho, the Derry-O
The farmer takes a wife

In the next verse, exchange the words "farmer" for "wife." Carry on through the list of characters. For example, after wife comes child. (The wife takes a child.) Then move on to nurse, then dog, then cat, then mouse, and finally cheese.

Human Knot
Number of players: The more people you have the harder (and more fun) this challenge gets!

Everyone stands in a tight circle and puts their hands in the middle—all mixed up—then they randomly grab hands with other players. Once everyone has their hands matched up with someone else, everyone slowly tries to untie the human knot to form a large circle. But don't let go of anyone's hand! You might have people facing backwards in the circle, some people having to climb over each other to get in the 'right' spot so they're untangled. It can get crazy!

Charades
Number of players: 2 or more.

One player acts out a word, phrase, movie title, person, or pretty much anything they can think of and the rest of the group tries to guess what they are acting out. The player cannot speak or make any noises while acting out their charade. The player who guesses correctly gets to act out the next charade.

Here are a few ideas to get you started:
Drink
Swim
Driving
Man on the moon
Cat
Tree
Singing
Baby
Eating
School
Milking a cow
Making a cake
Birthday party
Fight
Snowman
Watching a movie
Building a sandcastle

Meow, Kitty, Meow
One player who is "it" sits in the middle of a circle, blindfolded. They are spun around three times. Then they point at the person in front of them and say, "Meow, Kitty, Meow." That person then meows and "it" tries to guess who the person is—they only have the person's voice as a hint!

Follow the Leader
Number of players: 2 or more. (Preschoolers love the sense of power that comes with this one!)

One person leads and the rest follow by doing what the leader is doing. Take turns.

Follow the Leader Guessing Game
Number of players: 5 or more.

All players stand in a circle around one player. This player closes his/her eyes while the circle decides silently who is going to be the leader.

The player in the middle then opens their eyes and tries to figure out who the leader is as the game goes on. The leader secretly does things while the person in the middle is watching the group, trying to figure out who is the leader. When the leader does something (touch their nose, lift their foot, or whatever), the rest of the players quickly do the same thing while remaining in their circle—the faster they follow the leader, the harder it is to guess who the leader is.

When the person in the middle figures out who the leader is, the game is over. Start a new round!

Human Gumby
Who is Gumby? He was this crazy toy (and TV & movie character) that was invented in the 1950s that was super bendy.

Number of players: 4 (If you have more than four people, the extras can be the audience.) This is a fun improv game for older kids.

Two players are Gumby and the other two players are the controllers. The Gumbies stand still and do not move unless the controllers move them. (One controller for each Gumby.) The controllers gently arrange their Gumby's arms, legs, and head.

While the controllers are moving the Gumbies around, the two Gumbies have a conversation that makes sense with what their bodies are doing.

Add a Line Poems
Someone starts a poem by writing down a line. The next person adds a line, and the poem goes from person to person until you have a whole poem.

Variation: Cover all the lines except the last written line. This way the players can only see the last line and not the whole poem. Watch how the poem changes and changes!

Hint: Not all poems have to rhyme.

Switch a Line

Read a sentence from one story, then have a friend read a sentence from a different story. Take turns. Sometimes it sounds pretty silly! And sometimes it really actually kind of almost works.

Heads Up, Seven Up

Number of players: Lots and lots! 15 or more.

7 players are chosen to be at the front. The rest of the players put their heads down and cover their eyes. These players stick one thumb up. Each of the 7 walk around and touch one person's thumb. If a player's thumb was touched, they put their thumb down. The 7 then return to the front.

Those who had their thumb touched now try to guess who touched their thumb. If they guess right, they trade places with the person up front for the next round.

Players only get one guess. Once everyone has guessed, a new round begins.

Variation: If you don't have many players, you can have 3 people up front instead of 7.

Lonely Ghost

Number of players: 5 or more. You will need: one playing card for each player. One of the cards needs to be a joker.

Each player is dealt one card (face down). Everyone glances at their card.

The player who got the joker is the lonely ghost. This player will try to make the other players into ghosts by winking at them. The trick is to have no one notice the wink except the player being winked at. Once winked at, a player must count to 5 in their head and then say, "You Got Me." They are now out of the game.

If a player thinks they know who the ghost is, they can ask, "Are you the lonely ghost?" If they guess correctly, they win. If they do not guess correctly, they are out of the game.

If the ghost makes everyone else into ghosts without being caught, they win the game. Only the ghost is allowed to wink.

Improv Freeze Tag
Number of players: 5 or more.

Improv/Improvisation is a form of drama/acting. Instead of having a script to tell the actors and actresses what to do, the actors and actresses make it up as they go. It can be silly and also very challenging!

2 or 3 players (actors) stand on "stage" and improvise a conversation or activity for the audience.

Once the stage actors get going, an audience member can yell, "freeze!" The actors then freeze and the audience member who stopped the action takes someone's place on stage. (That actor joins the audience.) The actors, including the new one, then continue on with the story they were making up. There can be as many freezes as the group wants or until the group wants to go with a new idea.

Ideas to get you started: a wedding, breaking up with a boyfriend, grocery shopping, meeting a new friend, digging a hole.

Honey, Please Smile
Number of players: 4 or more.

One player tries to make one of the other players smile. To do this, they need to go up to another player and say, "Honey, if you love me will you please smile?" They are not allowed to say anything else, but they can do something funny to try and make the person smile while they are saying their line.

The player who has been asked must reply, "I am sorry, but I don't love you." They can't smile. If they smile, they have to trade places and try to get other players to smile while saying the line "Honey, if you love me will you please smile?"

And on it goes. Is it easy or difficult?

Musical Chairs
Number of players: 5 or more. You will need: music, chairs (one for each player—minus two).

Place chairs in a circle, their seats facing out. One player is in charge of the music, the others are trying to get a chair to sit on when the music stops.

Put out one chair for everyone, minus one chair. For example, if you have 5 people, one is in charge of the music and 4 are playing, so you need 3 chairs. Without looking at the players, the player with the music randomly turns the music on and off. The rest of the players walk around the chairs while the music is going. As soon as the music stops, everyone tries to get a chair to sit on. Whoever is left without a chair when the music stops is out. After each round, take out a chair. Keep playing until there is only 1 player left.

Variation: Everyone tries to get in a hula hoop or on a towel when the music stops.

Go Fish
Number of players: 3-6. You will need: deck of playing cards.

The more players, the more challenging it will be to remember who has what cards.

Deal 7 cards, face down, to each player. (If players are small and have trouble holding that many cards, deal 5.) The rest of the cards can be placed face down in a draw pile or spread out as a fishing pond.

Players are trying to make pairs for all the cards in their hand. If players are dealt a pair (two of the same cards) they place them face down in front of them. The player who has the most pairs at the end of the game wins.

The player left of the dealer goes first. He or she asks one of the other players if they have a certain card. For example: if the player has a king, they can ask another player if they have a king. If that player they asked has a king, they must give it to the asking player. The asking player keeps asking for cards from other players until someone doesn't have what they ask for and replies, "Go fish." The player that asked for a card now picks a card from the deck (or pond) and the turn moves to the next player. (If the player picks up a card from the pile which makes a pair with a card they already have in their hand, they can put down their pair, but they don't get to pick up another card or keep going.)

If a player runs out of cards in their hand, they pick up five more from the pile (if there are enough—if there are no more cards in the pile to pick up, they are done playing). Play until all of the cards have been paired. The player with the most pairs, wins.

Spoons

You will need 4 or more players, a spoon for each player (minus one player), and a deck of cards.

Spoons are placed in the middle of the players where everyone can reach them. One spoon per player, minus one player. So, if you have 4 players, put out 3 spoons.

From the deck of cards, pull out 4 cards for each player. The 4 cards for each player need to be the same. (For example, pull out 4 jacks for Becky, 4 8s for Kenna, etc.) Shuffle all the cards together then deal each player four cards.

Players look at their cards. If all four of their cards are the same, they grab a spoon. As soon as one player grabs for a spoon, everyone else does, too. The player who doesn't get a spoon, is out of the game.

If nobody was dealt four cards all the same, everyone gives away one card by passing it, face down, to the player on their right. They then pick up the card they were given from the player on their left. They can keep it, or pass it along. Keep going until someone gets four the same.

Variation: Players, once out, stay out until there is only one player with a spoon left. They are the winner. (As players leave the game, remove a spoon.) Or simply start a new round each time so everyone plays every game and they either win or don't.

This is My Head

One player is "it." They start the game by pointing to a part of their body and saying, "This is my head." (They don't point to their head though! They point to a different body part.) The next player then points to their head and says "This is my_____" (Foot, hand, elbow or whatever.) The next person points to a new part and says, "This is my _____." (Whatever the last person pointed to.) It gets confusing! See how far you can go before someone gets mixed up. (Being mixed up would be saying the RIGHT body part as you point to it!) Example:

Player 1: Points to knee and says, "This is my head."
Player 2: Points to head and says, "This is my foot."
Player 3: Points to foot and says, "This is my ear."
Player 4: Points to ear and says, "This is my ear." WRONG. You're out! (Crazy, isn't it?)

Duck, Duck, Goose
Number of players: 5 or more.

All players sit in a circle, facing in. One player walks around the outside of the circle and tags each player by touching them on the head while saying "duck." If they say "goose" instead of "duck" that player must jump up and run around the circle in the opposite direction that the tagger is going. Both players are racing for the empty spot in the circle where the goose was sitting. Whoever gets to the spot first and sits down, stays, and the other player goes around the circle tagging people as "duck" or "goose." If there is a tie, the goose gets to stay in the circle and tagger tries again with a new player.

Human Ping Pong Ball
Number of players: 6-10

One player is the ping pong ball. The rest of the players form a tight circle around them.

The ball **must** stand up tall and stiff like a board with their arms crossed over their chest with their hands up on their shoulders. Once ready, the ball slowly leans forwards, backwards or sideways by only bending their ankles. When the ball gets close to someone in the circle, they reach out and gently push the ball back towards center. The ball then goes in another direction.

Safety First: Make sure the circle is nice and tight.

Telephone
This game is best if you have 5 players or more players.

Have everyone sit in a circle. One player makes up a sentence—silly sentences are good—like, "On Sundays giraffes walk sideways in peanut butter." They whisper their sentence in the ear of the next player. That player repeats what they heard to the next player, and on and on until it reaches the last player.

The sentence can only be whispered to a player _once_. If someone forgets or doesn't hear it all, they have to repeat the sentence to the next player the best they can. The last player in the circle says the sentence out loud and the player who made up the sentence tells everyone what the sentence really was. Sometimes it is _very_ different!

Would you Rather
Ask your friends questions where they have a choice between two things. Start your sentence with "Would you rather…?" Then ask them silly, serious, or gross things. For example, you could ask, "Would you rather eat a booger or a worm?" Or "Would you rather jump out of an airplane with a parachute or sail in the air behind a boat?"

LITERARY PLAY

Play provides comfort and reassurance as well as reduces stress.

David Elkind
The Power of Play

Scientists know that playing naturally helps develop several areas of the childhood brain. This includes areas responsible for speech, reading, math, social skills, self-awareness, and overall intelligence. While the activities in this section may feel as though they are closer to something "educational" and prevent the dreaded summer holiday "intellectual slide" educational experts worry about, they are still a form of play and help build skills—as does all play. The difference between play activities and structured activities (which can be stress inducing in young children) is whether or not children can impose their own rules and ideas upon the activity. Can they spend as much time on the activity as they please? Can they make it their own? Can they change it into something entirely different?

In this section's activities I hope your children take the "opportunity to explore their environment freely" (David Elkind author of *The Hurried Child*) and place their own rules and ideas upon these activities. I also hope they find them reassuring and comforting (play) rather than stress-inducing (work).

P.S. In a study Elkind mentions in his book *The Hurried Child* they found that children who were introduced to reading late (rather than early) were more enthusiastic and spontaneous readers. According to Elkind, when children were compared a few years after attending preschool, those who attended an academic program were no further ahead academically than their play-oriented preschool peers. However, those who attended an academic preschool were more likely to have higher test anxiety, lower self-esteem, as well as more negative attitudes toward school. (Do note that these results may be, in part, a result of parental expectations as parents who place their children in curriculum-based preschools are, in effect, choosing and prioritizing (unconsciously or consciously) structure over free play for their children. In other words, negative results may not simply be a product of curriculum-based preschools but rather be the result of a larger, overall picture—that of the child's lack of an unstructured free play environment.)

Research Your Dream Job
Do you need to live in a city or in the country for your dream job? Do you need to go to university or college? What does a person do all day at this job? Do they travel? Do they sit behind a desk? What does it pay? Find out!

Create a Bucket List
Summer vacation must-do activities? Things to do before you grow up? Things to do as a family? Places you want to travel to? Create a list!

Hint: Are your kids too young to write out their list? Grab a travel magazine or newspaper and have them cut out photos of the things they're interested in.

100 Word Story
Can you write a short story in exactly 100 words?

Invent a New Language
Make up funny words as well as definitions for them. Have you read the book *Frindle* by Andrew Clements? This is an excellent example of a made up word changing the world! (For pretend of course, but I'm sure it happens in real life, too. Maybe.)

Make up Definitions for Words You Don't Know
Look in the dictionary for a word you don't know. Don't look at the definition until you have made your own. It can be silly or serious. Did you make up the right definition by accident?

Book Swap
Have you read all your books? Trade books with your friends.

Hint: Ask your parents if it is okay first.

Make a Crossword Puzzle
You will need: graphing paper, pen, and a ruler.

Hint: You can also find templates online as well as programs that will organize and build the crossword based on the words and hints you put into the program.

Try: http://www.discoveryeducation.com/free-puzzlemaker/

Make a Word Search
You will need: graphing paper, a pen.

Graphing paper will help keep your letters evenly spaced. Start by writing in your hidden words, then fill the empty spaces with random letters.

Hint: You can also find templates online as well as programs that will organize and build your word search based on the list of words you type into the program.

Try: http://www.discoveryeducation.com/free-puzzlemaker/

Read a Comic Book/Graphic Novel/Manga
If you are tired of your comics/graphic novels/manga/novels, trade with a friend (you may need to ask you parents first).

Bookcrossing
Bookcrossing is a group of strangers sharing books online in a treasure hunt sort of way.

Find a book you don't want any longer and are willing to "release it into the wild." Print a bookcrossing sticker off the bookcrossing website and glue it into your book along with a tracking number you also get from the site.

Drop your book off somewhere like a waiting room, bus, zoo, or anywhere someone might find it and take it home.

Then go to the bookcrossing site and post where you left your book—make sure you have your tracking number and the title of the book ready to type in.

Wait and see who picks it up. You can watch your book's journey as it passes from person to person. (As people find bookcrossing books, they post notes on the site—but not always. Some books get picked up by non-members who don't track the book. Fear not! They're just as likely to enjoy the book!)

Want to find books that have been released? You can also sign up for local update notices by email. Bookcrossing will then email you a list of books that have been released near you so you can try and find them—if someone hasn't beaten you to it!

More info: www.bookcrossing.com

Make Up a Story
You can make it up in your head, write it down, or tell it to someone.

Family Tree
A family tree is a list of the people in your family. Grandparents are one branch of your tree. Then, add branches from their main branch to your parents, aunts and uncles (also the children of your grandparents). Make another branch for the children of your parents (you).

Invisible Writing

You will need: lemon juice, squeeze bottle, paper, candle (blow dryer), and an adult's help.

Write a letter or draw a picture with lemon juice (pour the lemon juice in a squeeze bottle with a tiny squirt hole or brush it onto your paper with a paintbrush).

Safety First: Once the lemon juice has dried, ask a parent to hold the paper over a candle, just close enough that the heat makes the lemon turn brown. As it turns brown, you will be able to see what you wrote. (Sometimes a blowdryer works well, too. Just be careful—blowdryers can get hot enough to light paper on fire if left on "hot" for too long!)

Hint: You can buy invisible ink pens that write invisible and when you color over them with its partner pen, it reveals the words. I've also heard that egg whites or milk work well as "ink" and appear when the paper is heated up—cooking the egg or milk and turning it brown—just like with the lemon juice. I haven't tried it, so if you do, let me know if it works!

Letter to Yourself

Pretend you're a stranger, but that this stranger knows you. As this stranger, write a letter to yourself. What does this person think of you? Do they want to tell you a funny story about yourself from an outsider's point of view? What do they like about you?

Future Self

Write a letter to your future self. What do you like doing today? What do you think you will be doing when you open your letter in the future? Don't forget to write the date on your letter as well as an "open" date on the envelope.

This letter would be a great addition to your time capsule—instructions found in the Construction Crafts section.

Send Yourself a Postcard

Do you like getting mail? Mail yourself something and see how long it takes to get to you. Don't have a postcard, make one! (Find instructions in the Artistic Play section.)

Learn to Say Something in Another Language

You can ask someone to teach you, borrow language audiobooks from the library, learn from a language dictionary, or look a phrase or word up online.

Learn a New Word
Open the dictionary to any page and find a word you don't know. Or look up a word you have heard or read but don't know what it means. Try and use your new word three times today. My favorite word? Pristine. That one has been the word of the day in our household many, many times because it's fun and we like to use it in silly ways.

Fan Mail
Fan mail is a letter to someone you admire. If you want to send it to someone famous, you can probably find their fan mail mailing address with some help from a librarian or the famous person's fan website.

Write a Letter to Your Favorite Teacher
Tell them why they are your favorite teacher. Is there something they do that makes you smile, or makes your day? Are there activities you really like in class? Do they have a special way of teaching that makes learning easy and fun for you?

Thank-you Letters
Did you receive a gift recently? Why not write a letter to the person saying how much you liked the gift. They are sure to appreciate it!

If you didn't get a gift recently, but someone did something that made you feel good, write them a thank you letter. They'll be delighted!

Write to the Government
Tell the government what you think. You can write to the municipal government (local— like your town or county), the provincial/state government or to the federal government. You can get the addresses you need from the library or find it on a government website.

Horoscope
A horoscope is a prediction of what your upcoming week or month will be like based on your birthdate. You can find horoscopes online, in some magazines or newspapers. Don't like it? Make up a better one!

Write a Book Review
Leave a review online for a book you just read. Hey, you can start with this one! What do you like about the book? What don't you like? Who do you think would enjoy the book? Book reviews don't have to be super long and they can be super fun, too! (Not like at school.) Some people even make video book reviews. Wow!

Why I'm AWESOME!
Make a list of all the reasons why it is great to be you.

My Favorites List
Ideas: What is your favorite ice-cream? What is your favorite thing to do? What is your favorite time of year? What is your favorite color? What is your favorite book?

My Pet-Peeves List
What bugs you? What don't you like? Write it down!

Interview a Friend
What are their favorite colors? What are they afraid of? If they could grow up to be anyone in the world, who would it be? Who is their favorite famous person? Interview them as though you were on a talk show and didn't know these things about your friend. Bet you learn something new about them!

Interview Turnaround
Have a friend interview you (ask questions). BUT instead of answering the questions as YOU, you answer as THEM. Can you do it?

Words Inside Words
Take a long word such as "holiday" and see how many words you can make from scrambling the letters—you don't have to use them all. For example, can you find the word "day," "holy," and "laid" in the word "holiday?" Can you find more?

Can't think of any good words? Flip through a dictionary for inspiration.

You can play this game with a friend as well and see who can come up with the most words.

Research Your Favorite Things Online
What do you love? What are you curious about? Find out more! Fill that curiosity cup to the brim with new knowledge!

Search for Yourself on the Internet
Can you find yourself anywhere?

Safety First: Read my online safety tips before surfing the net.

I'm a Website

Type your name into a search engine and add things like .org, .com, and .ca to it to see if your name is a website. If you type your name directly into your browser, you could end up going to a site that's inappropriate so please check it out by using a search engine first—just to be safe.

Did you know my name is a website? www.JeanOram.com Know why? Because I made it! Tee hee.

Safety First: Read my online safety tips before surfing the net.

Let's...

- Read
- Speed Read
- Read Upside Down
- Read the Local Paper for Ideas on What to Do Today
- Write with Your Opposite Writing Hand
- Memorize Your Favorite Poem
- Memorize Your Favorite Movie Lines
- Memorize Funny Lines from Your Favorite Book
- Make Your Own Newspaper
- Write to a Pen Pal (Or get one!)
- Write to a Friend
- Look Through Your Mom and Dad's Old Yearbooks
- Find Your First Name in the Newspaper
- Write in a Diary/Journal
- Change Your Signature
- Write Words Backwards
- Write a Poem
- Do a Word Search
- Do a Crossword Puzzle
- Create Your Own Comic
- Start Your Own Newsletter
- Write a Play
- Make a Photo Slideshow of Your Family Vacation (Add cool captions, too!)

CITIZENSHIP PLAY: OUT OF THE GOODNESS OF YOUR HEART

> Play fosters empathy and makes it possible to form complex social groups.
>
> Stuart Brown
> Play

Play naturally induces empathy and a regard for others. While imaginary play allows us to put ourselves in another person's shoes, group play teaches sharing, and roughhousing play helps create empathy. The activities in this section build on the developmental impact of those free play activities and boost it up another level. Why? Because sometimes it just feels *really* good to do something nice for someone else. (And that can increase one's feelings of self-worth.)

Giveaway
Find something you don't use any longer or something you've outgrown. You might find one item or you might find a whole box! Check with your parents before you give it away though.

Just Because
Make someone a gift… just because! (See the Artistic Play section for ideas.)

Environmentalist Action
Do something good for the environment. We only have one planet earth and need to treat her well. What can you do that would help her out? A few ideas to help you get started: recycle, compost, plant a tree, and buy products with the least amount of packaging.

Good Deeds
A good deed is something you aren't paid or asked to do, but it will help someone out.

Ideas: carry someone's groceries, bag or books, or hold the door for someone, or shovel someone's sidewalk, or wash their windows, or water their flowers, or walk their dog, or… what else can you do?

Help Your Parents
What are your parents doing right now? Do they need help? Helping others can make someone's day as they get help with a tough task, but it can also teach you things that will help you out later in life. Plus, it's a nice thing to do and may bring you closer!

Charity Work
Charities are groups of people trying to do good in the world for animals, the environment, or others who simply need help. Charities aren't businesses and need money and help so they can help others. Want to help? You could raise money for a local charity (lemonade stand anyone?), or simple donate your time—charities always need helpers!

Pet Therapy
Pet therapy is when animals visit people who are not well. The cuddles from a friendly well-behaved pet help them feel better. Some places that might allow pet therapy are senior citizen and rehabilitation homes. Make sure you check to see if it is okay to bring your pet. Also check to see if your pet is suitable for visits.

Pick up Garbage
Take a garbage bag to the park, roadside ditches, school yard, or other places and clean up.

Safety First: Get some adult help for this one as some garbage you're parents won't want you touching without gloves, etc. So, it's best to check with them first. (Plus, you might get some help from them making it more fun!)

Get a Job
You could get a paper route, mow someone's lawn, babysit, work in a store…

Volunteer
Some organizations need help on a regular basis (like every week), while others need people for a one-time event such as a fundraiser. You can also offer to help someone out for free.

A few more…
- Give a Massage
- Help a Neighbor
- Give a Gentle Back Scratch

Musical Play

MUSICAL PLAY

According to Stuart Brown (author of *Play: How it Shapes the Brain, Opens the Imagination, and Invigorates the Soul*), play is pleasurable. It energizes and enlivens us as well as renews a natural sense of optimism while opening us up to new possibilities. Not only that, it shapes the brain in ways that makes us smarter and more adaptable. It also lies in the core of creativity and innovation. Play is our truest expression of individuality. That sounds a lot like we're talking about the benefits of musical play, doesn't it?

Let's dive in. (Oh, and in case you haven't heard, there is a link between musical knowledge and math scores. You have musical experience... your math scores go up. How about that?)

Change the Lyrics
Do you have a favorite song? Change the words to create a new song.

Gargle a Song
Can you hum a song while gargling? Try it! It's sounds crazy but it isn't as difficult as it sounds—just be careful not to breathe in that mouthful of water!

Make a Musical Instrument
An upside down pail can be a drum. A shoebox can be a guitar: stretch rubber bands over the opening. Hmm. What other instruments can you make?

Sing "The Song that Never Ends"—Loudly
Never heard of it? It goes like this:
This is the song that never ends,
It goes on and on my friend.
People started singing it, not knowing what it was,
Now they're forever singing it because,
This is the song that never ends...
(Keep singing it over and over, and over…)

Lip-sync
Put on your favorite music and move your lips to the lyrics—but don't actually sing out loud.

Air Band
An air band is a band that pretends they are playing instruments and singing the lyrics to their favorite songs, but all they do is act! An easy way to be a super star!

Listen to New Music
Tune into a radio station that you don't normally listen to.

Water Glass Instrument
Take several water glasses and add different amounts of water. Tap the glasses lightly with a metal spoon. The different water levels will result in different tones. See if you can play a song by tapping on the glasses.

Musical Statues
Everyone dances and when the music stops, everyone freezes. Who is the best statue?

Singing Glasses

Make a glass sing. Dampen the edge of a water glass or wine glass. Glide your finger around the edge until it starts to sing. Not working? Try more or less water on your finger as well as try pressing harder or lighter.

I've got the rhythm, have you got the blues?

- Make Actions for a Song
- Practice Playing an Instrument
- Learn to Play an Instrument
- Make a Mixed CD or Playlist
- Dance
- Make a Dance Routine
- Listen to Music
- Write a Song
- Make a Cheerleading Routine
- Sing "If You're Happy and You Know It" As Loud As You Can
- Sing the Alphabet Backwards
- Sing Every Song You Know
- Start a Band/Join a Band
- Whistle/Learn to Whistle

Guess the Tune

One person plays part of a song and you try to guess the song's artist (the band) and the title (song name).

Make a Shaker

This is a great toy for toddlers and it can also be a really neat musical instrument for your band.

Fill a plastic water bottle, or small plastic container with items such as buttons, beads, coins, rocks, or popcorn seeds. Shake away!

Safety First: Tape or glue the lid on the container (to prevent choke hazards for little ones). Also use this shaker under supervision as sometimes kiddos can open shakers despite our best attempts to lock them up.

Music Bingo

Write numbers on separate pieces of cardboard. (You will want the same number of cardboard pieces as there are players.) Write the same numbers that are on the cardboard down on squares of paper to place in a hat or bowl. Everyone dances around the squares on the floor. When the music stops everyone tries to get on a piece of cardboard. (One person per square.)

The person stopping the music then pulls one number from the hat. The player who is standing on that number is out of the game. Awww. They take that number (and cardboard) with them.

Super Loud Whistle

Place two fingers in your mouth to make the loudest whistle EVER!

I really wish I knew how to do this one. I've read about ten different methods and tried them all and I only got lightheaded from blowing so hard. And I may have spit on myself, too. Yeah, I have no super whistle magic. Do you have the magic?

Here's what I learned. Let's see if it works for you: Pull your lips over your teeth like you're pretending to be an old man. Push your pointer finger and thumb together, forming a circle. Place them over your old man lips, and in your mouth up to your first knuckle—you want that much of your fingers resting in your mouth (maybe wash your hands first).

Now close your mouth around your fingers so there is only a gap for air to escape between your fingers. Next, do some magic with your tongue. Curl it up and blow.

Did it work? Yeah, didn't work for me, either. Wait! It did! Awesooooome. Do it again! Do it again!

Word Dance

Everyone writes one word on a piece of paper and sticks it in a hat or bowl. Everyone chooses one word. Then everyone comes up with a dance—to the same music—based on their chosen word. Isn't it amazing how many different dances can be made for one song?

Ribbon Dance

Dance with ribbons, streamers, or scarves. Fast music, slow music… How does it change your dancing and the way the ribbon flows?

Numbers
Play

NUMBERS PLAY

Because children are spending so much time in front of the television, as well as other screens, there is little time for exercising their predisposition for fantasy, imagination, and creativity—the mental tools required for success in higher level math and science.

David Elkind
The Power of Play

According to the authors (Kathy Hirsh-Pasek, Roberta Michnick Golinkoff, & Diane Eyer) of *Einstein Never Used Flashcards,* intellectual play enhances intellectual curiosity and mastery. Or as Ronald Jarrel simply says, "Play is vital to the development of children's mathematical thinking." (And it doesn't even have to be math games. All play is good for the brain.)

Let's put the math back into play. Um, the play back into math? Either way you do it, counting and math is everywhere! You'll be developing math skills without even realizing it as you breeze through these fun number games.

Time Yourself
How fast can you walk? Run? Do the dishes? Put on your pajamas? Get your homework done? Run up the stairs? Drive your brother or sister nuts?

How Far Can You Walk in a Straight Line?
To make it extra challenging, spin around until you are dizzy, then try walking in a straight line. Can you walk further dizzy or not dizzy? Is it the same distance every time?

Measure Yourself
How tall are you? How long is your hand? How big is your ankle? How long are all of your toes?

Challenge yourself...
- How Far Can You Walk on Your Hands?
- How Long Can You Hold Your Breath?
- How Far Can You Hop on One Foot?
- How Far Can You Jump?
- Count Your Teeth
- Count Bugs and Other Creepy Crawly Insects
- Find a Coin From the Year You Were Born
- Count to 1000
- Find 10 Red Things in Your Room

Count Vehicles
Waiting for someone? In the car? Near a street? Looking out your front window while waiting for Grandma to arrive? Count vehicles. How many vehicles go by in a minute? Did you see more vans or more cars or more trucks? Compare this with what goes by at your friend's house or at another location.

Speed Clock
Start at 1 o'clock and work your way around the clock, adding all the numbers. See how fast you can go. For example: start at 1 o'clock, then move on to 2 o'clock. So: 1 + 2 = 3. Your answer is 3, so move on to 3 o'clock. 3 (your answer from the last round) + 3 (the next o'clock on the clock) = 6. The next question will be 6 + 4 (o'clock) = 10. Next: 10 + 5... and on you go around and around.

Dare to Compare
Let's face it. As a kid you end up waiting in a lot of boring places. The dentist's office. The mall. The tire shop. The hardware store. Your sibling's sports practice. I could go on and on. Let's dare to compare!

Is it winter? How many people are wearing boots? How many are wearing shoes?

Is it summer? How many people are wearing shorts? How many aren't wearing shorts? Anyone wearing a hat? Are they men or women?

What else can you compare?

Magazine Picture Find and Count
Pick an item, like a tree, or a person smiling. See how many you can find in an entire magazine. Did you lose count?

Count Windows
How many windows are in your home?

Count Clocks
How many clocks are in your home?

Count Pictures
You can count paintings, photographs, posters...

Count Doors

How many doors are in your home. Now… here's the question. Should you count closets and cupboard doors, too?

Count Things to Sit on

How many things are there for sitting on in your home?

Count Plants

How many plants (real and fake) are in your home?

Squares

This one is a bit trickier and is great for older kids.

Take a grid of dots—ten dots across in a line, ten down all in a line. Fill it in to make a grid that has 100 dots (10 x 10). (You might be able to find some online so you don't have to draw it out yourself.)

One player draws one line between two dots. The next player draws another line between two dots. The goal is to draw a line that closes a "box" to make a square. So four dots— four corners of your square box.

When you close a box, you get another turn. As well, mark the box with your initial so they can be counted at the end. The player that has formed the most boxes wins.

TRAVEL GAMES

Free play develops self-regulatory skills, the ability to resist impulses, exert self-control and discipline... In fact, self-regulation is a better predictor of school success than IQ.

Gabrielle Principe
Your Brain on Childhood

Did someone say road trip? A most excellent time to get bored! Have no fear, this section will keep your kids entertained (while unwittingly developing skills such as teamwork, communication, and visual identification skills). These activities will not only help the miles speed by, but will help decrease parental/driver insanity.

Also be sure to check out the next chapter on Word Games as they are *perfect* for playing in the car. Finally, there's more to do than ask, "Are we there yet?"

P.S. Many of these games can be played as a group, or individually.

———————————

Rain Drop Races
If you've got foggy windows, wipe the glass until droplets form. Race two drops to see which one reaches the bottom of the window first.

If it's raining, see which raindrops on the outside of the window reach the bottom first.

Wave at Everyone You See
How many wave back?

I Spy
One player spies (sees) something without telling anyone what it is. They say, "I spy with my little eye something that is (and they name the color of the item they saw)." The other players try to guess what has been spied. If you are travelling in a car, it is best to choose items that are in the car that everyone can see.

Car Ride I Spy Booklet
Cut pictures and words out of a magazine and glue them on a piece of paper. Check things off as you find them on your trip. For example, pictures of a dog, a bus, a crosswalk sign, the word "exit," the letter "X," etc.

Travel Journal
A travel journal can take on many different forms. It can be a diary about the trip, or it can include drawings of places you have seen, photographs, ticket stubs, maps, brochures, and other items you collect during the trip. Or it can be all of the above!

Where is the Fairy Hiding?
Ready to use your imagination? One player pretends they're a tiny fairy hiding in the car. (The fairy is only about an inch tall. For younger children, you can use a toy figurine as an example for how small the fairy is in order to make the game easier for them as their spatial skills may be still developing making this a tricky game.)

The first player chooses a spot where their imaginary fairy is hiding in the car. They give no hints while the other players try to guess where the fairy is hiding by asking "yes" or "no" questions. Example: Are you in the front passenger seat? Yes. Are you near the floor? No. Are you in Mom's hood? Yes.

The player who guesses it right goes next.

Variations: Got kids who aren't into fairies? Change it! It doesn't matter who is hiding as long as everyone knows how big it is.

Punch Buggy
Whenever you see a Volkswagen Beetle you yell "Punch buggy, _____" (name the car's color). Then gently punch (or nudge) the person beside you on the arm.

Pick and Count
Pick something to count (like trees, red cars, dumpsters, cows) and see how many you find.

Boost the challenge: Set a time limit, such as 5 minutes. Or play against someone on the other side of the car. See who can find the most by only looking out their side of the car.

Find 10
Pick something and then try and find 10 of them. Did you pick red cars? Waterfalls? Semis? Yellow signs?

Find It!
Pick something specific like a church, hospital, flag, blue semi. Keep looking until someone finds it.

License Plate Find It
Pick a number or letter and try to find it on a license plate. Playing with a friend? See who can find it first.

License Plate Phrases

Make a phrase or word from the letters and numbers on a license plate. For example: license plate "RSN 542" could become Really Silver Nickels or Reason #542.

Collect States & Provinces

Look at the license plates on the vehicles around you. See how many different places you can find. Can you find all the provinces and territories or all of the states? See who finds the most.

License Plate Numbers

See how high you can count by finding numbers on license plates. Start with finding 1, then watch the next plate for 2…

Alphabet License Plate Game

Most license plates have numbers and letters. Search for the whole alphabet in license plates. Start by looking for the letter "A." Once you have found that, go on to letter "B." On you go through the whole alphabet—go in order!

Boost the challenge: Take only one letter from each license plate. In other words, you can't take the letters "A" and "B" from the same license plate.

Stop or Thru

Players try to guess whether the traffic light will stop them (yellow or red) or let them through (green) by saying, "Stop," or "Through."

How Long Will it Take

Look at something up ahead on the road you're on and that your vehicle will pass. Guess how many seconds it will take before you pass it.

Blind How Long Will it Take

Play the game above, only with your eyes closed. Try to open your eyes at the exact moment that you pass the item you chose. See if you can open your eyes at the exact right moment. Are you good at it? Or is it hard? I'll bet this one gets tricky in the city with stop and go traffic!

Next Color Vehicle

This game is great for a quiet or winding road. Try and guess what color the next vehicle that comes into sight will be.

Next Kind of Vehicle

Try and guess what kind of vehicle will come into sight next. Truck? Car? Minivan? SUV? Semi? Or guess the make—Dodge? Ford? Chevrolet? Lexus? BMW?

Sign Alphabet Game

Get the whole alphabet by searching for letters on signs you pass. Start with "A" and work your way through the alphabet.

Boost the challenge: Take one letter from each sign. In other words you can not take A, B, and C from one sign. As well, you have to get the letter Q (a hard one) before you move on to the next letter, R.

Sign Numbers

Each player counts to 10. BUT they can only get there by finding the numbers they need on signs they pass in the car.

Work together to get to 10 or play against each other to see who gets to 10 first.

Tip: This game can also be played alone.

Boost the challenge: Take one number from each sign. In other words you can't take 1, 2, and 3 from one sign. You have to find three separate signs.

Alphabet Game

Find things outside the car that start with each letter of the alphabet. Start with A. See an apple tree? Next try something that starts with B. Keep going through the whole alphabet.

Banana

Who spotted a yellow vehicle?

Players get points every time they see one—but only one point per vehicle so the first person to spot it gets the point.

Variation: Too hard to find yellow? Change the game! How about Apple—find red vehicles. Set a time limit. Or give points based on how much red there is on a vehicle. Be creative and make this game your own.

Who Are They

As you pass another vehicle use your imagination to try and guess what sort of person is driving. Be creative and try to imagine what that person is like and how they came to be there. You can be silly or serious.

You can play this game alone, or with others. If playing with others, each person can take their own turn without interruption as they create a history for the other driver. Or, players can build off of each other's stories and ideas.

Variation: Guess who lives in a house or works in a business you pass.

Round Up

This game evolved out of a cow game my husband and I made up the summer we got married and were doing a lot of driving across the prairie between university and my hometown.

Each player chooses a side of the road. They will try to spot as many cows as they can on their side of the road. That means they can't count cows they see on the other player's side. If a player sees a dog (on either side of the road), and says "Cow round-up" first, they add the other player's cow total to their own (but the other player doesn't lose points). If a player sees a semi truck with a cow hauler, and is the first to say, "Cows went on a trip," the other team loses all their cows and has to start at 0 again. If a player sees a grocery store and is the first to say, "Cows got fed," they add 50 cows to their total. If one player is behind the other player in points and they see a food truck of any kind (like a grocery truck, fast food truck, beverage truck) they can yell "Ketchup" and they will catch-up in points and be even with the other player again.

Variation: Change this game depending on where you live. Instead of cows, try gas stations. Each player tries to spot as many gas stations as they can on their side of the road. If they see a gas truck, they say "Fill up" and get 10 points. If they see a tow truck and are the first one to say, "Out of gas" the other team loses all of their points. If a player sees a gas station billboard and says, "Gas Bonus," they add the other team's points to their own, but the other team doesn't lose their points.

What other variations can you think of?

Rest Stop Track Meet

One person chooses an activity for the next rest stop (or gas station stop) whether it is to run to the nearest tree, do ten jumping jacks, or play five minutes of Frisbee or soccer. At the next rest stop, someone else chooses. Not only will this help relieve the ants-in-your-pants that builds up in small kids, but it will help keep the driver stay alert, too.

Guess What I Saw

As the vehicle drives along, the "it" player chooses something they just passed. They can then give other players a clue such as the number of letters in the word, its color, or size.

Playing with younger kids? Make it easier. For example, if your chosen item was a black dog, you might start your turn with: "Guess what I saw? It's black." Or "Guess what I saw? It's an animal."

You can set a time limit, a number of guesses, or the number of miles or kilometers traveled to keep the guesses from going on forever. The player who guesses correctly gets to go next.

Road Bingo

Draw a bingo card that has five squares across and five squares down for a total of 25 squares.

Draw different things you might see on your trip in each square, except the very middle square which is your "free" square just like on a regular bingo card. Make slightly different cards for each player on your road trip. Picture ideas: tree, plane, train, something red, emergency vehicle, fluffy cloud, highway route sign, tractor trailer…

Just like in regular bingo, each player tries to cross out their squares in either a line, diagonal, or blackout (all squares) to create a bingo—however, instead of someone calling out items, you have to find them as you drive past them! Whoever gets bingo first, wins.

Hint: Try making these cards on your computer and use clipart images in the squares (or cut them out of a travel magazine and paste them on). You can make each card a bit different, save them on your computer, then reprint them as needed.

Car Ride Scavenger Hunt
Look for the items listed below (or make your own list) while riding in the car. Play alone, as a team, or against someone else to see who finds all the items first.

bridge
cow
blue minivan
tree shorter than the vehicle you are riding in
person with white or grey hair who is driving another vehicle
semi truck
motor home
bus
sign with the letter 'F' on it
speed limit sign
vehicle you think is speeding
fast food restaurant
overpass
red car
vehicle with an out of province/state license plate
vehicle that is for sale
vehicle that has a company name painted on the side of it
child riding in another vehicle
pedestrian

Boost the challenge: Find the items in the order they appear on the list. Good luck!

Pick a Car
One player picks a type of vehicle or make or model and everyone tries to find one. Can you do it? Can you share the same vehicle or do you have to spot a different one than the other players?

A few bonus activities...
- See Who Can Be Quiet the Longest
- Count Train Cars
- Follow Your Route on a Map
- Draw on Frosty Car Windows

I Spy Treasure Bag/Bottle Hide-and-Seek

This is a fabulous game for toddlers and preschoolers and is easy to make. You might want to make one for the car and one for the house!

Fill a small plastic drinking bottle with rice and a few trinkets such as buttons, coins, paperclips, old earrings, and anything else you can find that is small and interesting. Leave enough room in the bottle so you can twist and turn the bottle and have things move around, hiding some items and surfacing others. Trinket hide-and-seek!

Tip: Keep a photo list of the items hidden in the bottle. Your child tries to find all the objects on the list by turning the bottle or bag to make the item surface. Or, you can call out from the front seat things such as, "Can you find something round?" or "Can you find something blue?" (Or you might want to hold onto the list and ask them to find certain items.) You also may want to secure the lid with tape or glue so curious minds with monkey fingers don't open it in the car.

Variation: Handy at sewing? Sew up a bag with a plastic window (I found that the plastic zip up bags most linens come in work well—they are sturdy, but soft enough you can sew through them with your machine). Use stuffing beads (for making teddy bears) inside the bag instead of rice (rice will leave dusty debris over time).

WORD GAMES

> Imagination and fantasy play can help children deal with past demons as
> well as anticipate challenges in their future.
>
> David Elkind,
> The Power of Play

Many of these games are good for developing memory skills with a friend. Play them at
sleepovers, at birthday parties, or in the car.

In the Car I Read

Do you like to read? This is the game for people who love books… or at least can think of a lot of different book titles!

The first player says, "In the car I read _____ (book title)." The next player says, "In the car I read (they say the title mentioned by the first player, and _____ (add another book title)." The chain keeps going, growing, and growing as each player adds a book to the list. The first person who can't remember all of the titles is out of the game.

For example:
Player one: In the car I read *Harry Potter*.
Player two: In the car I read *Harry Potter* and *Gulliver's Travels*.
Player three: In the car I read *Harry Potter*, *Gulliver's Travels*, and *Walter the Farting Dog*.

Variation: Movie titles! In the car I watched…

Or vacation spots! In the car I drove to…

I'm Thinking of a Word

One player chooses a word (in their head), and the other players try to guess what the word is. Hints can be given! Maybe it rhymes with "fog" or "it has five letters in it and Dad really likes it."

Storytelling Chain

Group storytelling without any twists. Everyone makes up one line for the group story. So, one person starts the story by saying one sentence, then the next player takes over, adding their own line to the story. Once upon a time there was a girl…

Unfortunately-Fortunately

Take turns doing shared story telling, but switch between "unfortunately" and "fortunately" to start your sentences. For example:

First player: "Unfortunately our essay that was due next week is really due tomorrow morning."
Next player: "Fortunately, I have mine done."
Next player: "Unfortunately the teacher added an extra page."
Next player: "Fortunately, mine was two pages over."

And Then...
Number of players—however many you want!

One player starts a story. They start the story with one sentence, but add "and then..." at the end of their sentence. The next player then picks up the story and continues by adding one sentence, adding "and then..." to the end. (You can also say "but then" if it fits the story structure better or you want to change the story's direction.)

The story might go something like so:
Player one: I crossed the train tracks and then...
Player two: a train smashed into the truck behind me and then...
Player three: the people ran out and said "Whew, that was close." But then...

No Smiling
It's time to get silly!

Think of a silly phrase that would make you smile if it was your answer to everything anyone asks you. The sillier the better. For example, "dog breath" or "spider legs."

Ready? One person is "it" and can only use the silly phrase while the other players ask normal questions such as, "What is your favorite pizza topping?" Or "What is your favorite thing to wake up to in the morning?" The "it" player has to answer every question with the chosen silly phrase (ex. dog's breath) with a perfectly straight face. No smiling or they're out and it's someone else's turn.

One Minute Speeches
This game needs two or more people and a timer.

The timekeeper picks a topic for the "speaker" and keeps track of the time using a timer, clock or watch.

When the timekeeper says, "Go" the speaker must start talking about the chosen topic and can't stop until their 1 minute is up. No interrupting!

Topic Ideas: shoelaces, teddy bears, things that go bump in the night, things that fly, things I will do when I am famous, things that are blue.

Spelling Bee
Who can spell the most number of words correctly?

If I was a Billionaire
"If I was a billionaire I would buy…" But the player doesn't finish this sentence, just thinks of what they would buy. (Swimming pool, a plane, a million lollipops…) The rest of the players try to guess what it is that they would buy. Clues can be given out as needed.

My Neighbor's Dog
The first player says, "My neighbor's dog…" And then the dog does something that begins with the letter A. For example, "My neighbor's dog went to Albania."

The next player does the same thing, only uses a new word that starts with A. For example, "My neighbor's dog likes applesauce."

The game keeps going until one person can't think of something that begins with A. You then move on to things the neighbor's dog does that starts with the letter B.

You can play for points or simply play for fun. If playing for points, when a player can't think of something that begins with the letter currently in play and you have to move to the next letter in the alphabet, they get one point *against* them.

Guess the Number
One player picks a number in their head. The other player(s) try and guess what the number is. They can ask questions such as, "Is it higher than _____?"

For example: Is the number over 60?
No.
Is it an even number?
Yes.
Is it 20?
No.
Is it over 20?
Yes.
Is it 44?
Yes!

I'm Going on a Picnic/I'm Going on a Trip and I'm Taking

The more people playing, the more challenging this game becomes. One person starts by saying, "I'm going on a picnic and I am taking a…" (says something they're going to bring). Or you can start the game with the sentence, "I am going on a trip and in my suitcase I am packing…"

The next person repeats the sentence as well as what the other person is bringing, then adds something they are bringing. For example:

Player one: "I am going on a picnic and I am taking jelly beans."
Player two: "I am going on a picnic and I am taking jelly beans and pizza."

The first player to forget one the items from the growing list is out.

Variation: Players can only bring items that start with the same letter as their first name. For example, Jean can only bring things like, jelly beans, jam, and juice, but not oysters. As well, if playing with younger players, you can play a version where they don't have to remember what everyone is bringing—they just have to think something up to bring.

Apple Bear

Start with the letter "A." The first player says a word (any word!) that starts with A, and then the next player repeats it plus adds something to the list that starts with the letter B, and on and on through the alphabet you go until someone forgets something from the growing list.

Geography

Starting with the letter "A," one player has to name a country or town that begins with A. For example, Australia. The next player moves down the alphabet to B. The next player, C.

Variation: Want to make it harder? The place name has to *end* with the letter "A" instead of start with it. Oooh, that's tricky!

Someone We Know

One person thinks of a person the whole group knows. (Real or famous.) The others ask questions that can be answered "yes" or "no" in order to try and figure out who the person is. They keep narrowing it down and guessing until someone gets it right or they need a big hint.

What If

Think about what would happen if… an elephant ran the town instead of the mayor? What if aliens abducted your teacher? (What would school be like then?) What if you were famous or your parents were famous? What if your dog could talk?

There are no limits to "What if" questions.

Hint: Answering "what if" questions are a great way to start writing short stories and poems.

Remember That Time

We have a game in our family that makes reminiscing (see more on reminiscing in the Kids Stuff section) into a goofy game. One person says, "Remember that time? That was fun." Then the other people have to either try to guess which time they are remembering…

Remember That Time Make-Believe

Like the game above but when the other person says, "Remember that time? That was fun." The others say something goofy like, "Yeah, I remember that time. I can't believe you got your pants hooked on the very top of the CN Tower while skydiving and I had to fly a helicopter over to save you." The other person goes with it, building a silly story.

Question—Question

Two people have a conversation, but they can *only* ask questions. If playing with more than two players, switch players out as they mess up (they don't ask a question).

Here is an example:
Player one: How are you?
Player two: What do you mean?
Player one: What are you crazy?
Player two: No, are you?
Player one: Sometimes, but how are you?
Player two: I'm fine (and they are out because this isn't a question!).

Hint: The conversation doesn't always have to make *complete* sense.

Variation: Make it harder—players have to reply right away (no pause to think about what they are going to ask) or they are out.

Word Association
Two or more players.

One person says a word and the next person says the first word they think of. Fast! Fast! Then the next person says the first word they think of.

For example:
Player One: Dog
Player Two: Cat
Player Three: Tree
Player Four: Leaf
Player One: Hockey
Player Two: Cold
Player Three: Ice-cream
Player Four: Hungry

Add a Word
A friend says a word and then you say a word. Go back and forth until you have a sentence or a story.

You can also play this on paper—warning! It can get silly.

Add a Sentence
A friend says a sentence. You say their sentence then add your own. They then say the first two sentences and then add another one. Keep going until you begin to forget or your story is done.

Variation: This can be played on paper instead of out loud as well as played with more than 2 players. It can also be played where players do not repeat the sentences.

Animal, Vegetable, Mineral/20 Questions
This is a guessing game that needs at least two people.

One player chooses something that is an animal, vegetable, or mineral. They tell the other players (the guessers) whether the object is an animal, vegetable, or mineral, but they don't tell them what it is.

An animal includes humans, animals, extinct animals (such as dinosaurs) and fictional characters like Spiderman. A vegetable includes all plants, including things that used to be a living plant. For example, a wooden toy box used to be a tree, so it is a vegetable. A cotton T-shirt is also a vegetable because cotton grows on plants before it is picked, spun into thread, woven into fabric, then made into clothes. A mineral is everything that has never lived like rocks, metals, and plastics. Cars, mountains, glass and coins are minerals.

The guessing game begins! The guessers get 20 guesses in total (you can change it to more or less or even not keep track at all). The guessers must ask questions that have "yes" or "no" answers. The player with the object in mind can only answer "Yes" or "No" to any question asked.

For example:
Game Starts: "The object I am thinking of is an animal."
Guesser: "Is it bigger than me?"
"Yes."
Guesser: "Can it fly?"
"No."
Guesser: "Can I find it living in the mountains?"
"Yes."
Guesser: "Is it a bear?"
"No."
Guesser: "Does it have horns?"
"Yes."
Guesser: "Is it a big horn sheep?"
"Yes!"

Because, Because, Because
My four-year-old started this game in our family. Always eager to get a word in edgewise and maintain control of the conversation he starts telling us a story, then adds "because" and starts another sentence—because then it's harder to interrupt him, right? He once kept a sentence going for ten minutes! (Yep, I timed him.)

Example: I walked to the store because I wanted a chocolate bar because I was hungry because I didn't want an apple like Dad suggested because…

How long can you keep it going? (And it's okay if the story gets bumpy!)
Variation: Timed stories—you have to keep it going for thirty seconds OR you pass the story on to the next player after you say "because."

ONLINE SAFETY TIPS

While most of the activities in this book are unplugged play—unscripted play that gets back to the basics of childhood and uses very little technology, if any—a few of them involve computers or the online world. Therefore, I've provided a few online safety tips in this section as well as some science to help you decide how much plugged-in time you'd like in your household. First, the science…

The Impact of Computer and Video Games on Child Development

The good, the bad, and the ugly.

According to author David Elkind (professor in the field of child development), computer games have some benefits as well as drawbacks. On the positive side, computer games can engage children in active thinking, provide mental exercise as well as work on problem-solving. However, he also warns that computer games can take away opportunities to experience the real world—a place where children learn a great deal about themselves, social nuances, the natural world, and more. He reminds us that "real play is essential to healthy mental, physical, and social-emotional growth and development. The challenge is to find the right balance between screenplay and actual play."

As well, in a time where childhood obesity and depression and anxiety is reaching epidemic proportions, Stuart Brown points out that computer play is not only a sedentary activity but one that creates emotional arousal without a physical discharge. This results in children feeling antsy and unfocused. On top of that author Gabrielle Principe (a psychology professor who focuses on child cognitive development) notes that "researchers have found that young children who frequently play video games are four times more likely to develop myopia than children who regularly play outdoors."

Need a ray of hope? Gabrielle Principe notes that parents who police computer use can decrease the negative effects of computer use—computers can act as a tempting distraction that takes away from homework time which then leads to lower grades and reduced educational aspirations.

Online Safety Tips:
Never give out your real name, phone number, or address to people on the internet. If they have not been to your house and had supper with your family, consider them a stranger, no matter how much you think you know them.

Other personal information. Information like your school team names, hobbies, places where you hang out a lot—all of those kinds of things can lead someone to you. So be careful! (Other don'ts: Don't give out your teacher's names, school name, your age, teams or clubs you belong to, your grade, your family's names.

Be careful how much "non-personal" information you give out. Even though you might use a fake name, if you give details about the area you live or your life, you are giving out clues on how to find the real you. For example, if your town just had a huge snowstorm and five trucks drove off the road and you talk about it online, people might be able to find you (or your town) using that information.

People aren't always who they say they are. Maybe that 12-year-old you befriended is really a 40-year-old. Always be careful who you trust.

If you aren't sure if you should give out the information—don't. If in doubt about anything online, ask your parents.

Never meet someone you met online in real life—unless a parent comes with you.

If someone makes you feel uncomfortable online, stop and tell an adult.

***If anyone asks for the above information, stop the online conversation or leave the website and ask your parents or teachers whether it is okay to reply or not.

Play safe!

P.S. It's also a good idea to use a firewall and virus protector on your computer before you go surfing.

RESOURCES

Want to read more about child development and the importance of play?

Here are a few of the books I've read and loved. (Also includes the books and authors I've quoted in this book.). Many of these authors also have fantastic websites and/or blogs.

A Child's Work: The Importance of Fantasy Play (Vivian Gussin Paley, 2005.)

Einstein Never Used Flashcards: How Our Children Really Learn—And Why They Need to Play More and Memorize Less (Kathy Hirsh-Pasek, Roberta Michnick Golinkoff, & Diane Eyer, 2004.)

Free-Range Kids: How to Raise Safe, Self-Reliant Children (Without Going Nuts with Worry) (Lenore Skenazy, 2010.)

The Hurried Child: Growing Up Too Fast Too Soon (David Elkind, 2001.)

Last Child in the Woods: Saving Our Children from Nature-Deficient Disorder (Richard Louv, 2008.)

The Over-Scheduled Child: Avoiding the Hyper-Parenting Trap (Alvin Rosenfeld and Nicole Wise, 2001.)

Play: How it Shapes The Brain, Opens the Imagination, and Invigorates the Soul (Stuart Brown, 2010.)

Power of Play: How Spontaneous, Imaginative Activities Lead to Happier, Healthier Children (David Elkind, 2007. Also entitled *The Power of Play: Leaning What Comes Naturally.*)

Putting Family First: Successful Strategies for Reclaiming Family in a Hurry-Up World (William J. Doherty and Barbard Carlson, 2002.)

Under Pressure: Putting the Child Back in Childhood (Carl Honoré, 2008.)

Your Brain on Childhood: The Unexpected Side Effects of Classrooms, Ballparks, Family Rooms, and the Minivan (Gabrielle F. Principe, 2011.)

BEFORE YOU GO...

Do you need one more reason to allow your children to engage in play? How about this quote from the authors of *Einstein Never Used Flashcards*:

> Children who play more are happier. When children are happier, they tend to relate better to their peers and they tend to be more popular.

Thanks for reading. Happy playing!

Liked this book? Leave a review online or suggest it to your friends. The author thanks you (that's me)! Play on.

ABOUT THE AUTHOR

Jean Oram used to write lists of things to do for her friends when they couldn't decide what to do together. When her first child was less than a year old she took up her old habit again and began a list of free play ideas in case her daughter ever came to her with those dreaded words on her lips, "I'm bored." Within days she had hundreds of ideas. And eventually, this book was born. Her daughter is now a preteen and many of the activities in this book have been tested (or invented) in the Oram household.

Jean Oram is a *New York Times* bestselling romance author, mother of two, instigator of play, and a fun wife. She loves to spend time in the great outdoors getting dirty and playing. (She loves it when her kids join in.) She's worked as a library children's programmer, ski instructor, as well as beekeeper. She lives in Canada with her family and big shaggy dog.

Want more play? Believe it or not... I have more!

Check out my website and blog: www.itsallkidsplay.ca
Check out my pins on Pinterest: www.pinterest.com/jeanoram

Made in the USA
Monee, IL
26 November 2021

83138476R00136